AMERICAN TRAILS SERIES
XVIII

CAPPED ROCK, GUADALUPE CANYON, NEW MEXICO
*"One stupendous monument reared itself near the center of the glen ... one whose
grateful and stupendous outline pointed in the clear blue sky above, set at naught
all efforts at imitation, and which proudly proclaimed its Architect of Projector
Infinite in power as the rippling stream, the gorgeous, and leafy canopy
at its base, did His infinity in love and mercy"*
William W. Hunter, 62:9/15. Author photo, 1982

TO CALIFORNIA
ON THE
SOUTHERN ROUTE
1849

A History and
Annotated Bibliography

by
Patricia A. Etter
with a foreword by
Elliott West

THE ARTHUR H. CLARK COMPANY
Spokane, Washington
1998

To Paul, with love

"Alas, little dreamed we of the huge,
colossal *Elephant* we were about to see!"

Benjamin Butler Harris,
The Gila Trail, September 29, 1849

Printed in an edition of 750 copies
Designed by Robert Clark

Copyright 1998 by
Patricia A. Etter

LIBRARY OF CONGRESS CATALOG CARD NUMBER 98-35538
ISBN-0-87062-270-6

Etter, Patricia A., 1932—
    To California on the southern route, 1849 : a history and
annotated bibliography / Patricia A. Etter ; with a foreword by
Elliott West.
        p.   cm.—(American trail series ; 18)
    Includes bibliographical references and index.
    ISBN 0-87062-270-6
    1. Southwest, New–Description and travel.   2. Overland journeys
to the Pacific.   3. Trails—Southwest, New—History—19th century.
4. Frontier and pioneer life—Southwest, New.   5. Pioneers-
-Southwest, New—History—19th century.   6. Southwest, New-
–Description and travel—Bibliography.   7. Overland journeys to the
Pacific—Bibliography.   8. Trails—Southwest, New—History—19th
century—Bibliography.   9. Frontier and pioneer life—Southwest,
New—Bibliography.   10. Pioneers—Southwest, New—History—19th
century—Bibliography.   I. Title   II. Series.
F786.E88   1998
979'.02—dc21   98-35538
                                                                 CIP

CONTENTS

ILLUSTRATIONS

FOREWORD

The great overland migrations were some of the best documented episodes in American history. The hundreds of thousands of persons who traveled from the middle border to the Pacific coast in the mid-nineteenth century left behind many thousands of diaries, journals, and letters. This small library of testimony reveals in rich detail the difficulties, pleasures, occasional tragedies, and relentless grind of the journey. They tell, too, of the land and its changes. They open our eyes, usually unintentionally, to the crisis that the transcontinental passage brought to the native peoples inhabiting the plains, deserts, and mountains. The overlanders looked on this country as a barrier to endure and put behind them; the Lakotas, Cheyennes, Shoshoneans, Pimas, and others saw it as a homeland being threatened by the massive waves of people and animals that marched and grazed their way across it.

There is a curious imbalance to the historical treatment of the migration, however. Of the scores of published diaries and correspondence from the migration and the dozens of historical studies written about it, virtually all concern the pioneers who went westward via the Oregon-California trail. This route—up the Platt and forking beyond South Pass, with one road angling northwestward over the Blue Mountains to Oregon and the other going southwestward, across the Great Basin and over the Sierra Nevada to California—was indeed a busy continental thoroughfare that carried roughly a third of a million persons to the Pacific. It was the longest-lived passage: the first wagons rolled over the trails in the early 1840s and slackened seriously only after the Civil War. But the Oregon-California route was by no means the only one taken by the farmers, shopkeepers, doctors, thieves, lawyers, clockmakers, coopers, and dentists who trudged westward to seek (and occasionally actually find) their fortunes.

At least 20,000 persons rushed to California in 1849 by another way—a cluster of trails through the southwestern deserts, routes that had been used for many generations by native peoples and for decades by fur trappers and traders. Use of the Southern Route slacked off after the great rush, but it did not stop. This part of the story of the overland migration should appeal to us for all the reasons better known trails have drawn such attention. It was full of travails, adventures and grueling labor. Human nature at its bravest and most sordid was fully on display. The accounts open a unique window on a poorly documented place and time in western history, and they tell us something about the indigenous peoples and their gathering calamity. It all unfolded in what was surely one of the most challenging environments in North America.

Just why the Southern Route has been so neglected is an intriguing question. Probably fewer journals and diaries were written, per capita, than on the northern roads, in part because most desert travelers came from regions with the lowest literacy rates in the nation. By the time of the gold rush, the Platte River route was already well entrenched in the popular consciousness after eight years of highly publicized emigration to the Eden of the moment, Oregon's Willamette Valley. The northern routes passed through country rich in the emblematic residents of the mythic West; then and now, readers likely have been more interested in reading about herds of bison and Sioux and Pawnees, familiar tribes from journalistic accounts and dime novels, than about lizards and rattlesnakes, Pimas and Mohaves.

Whatever the reasons, the results have been unfortunate. Until now a revealing chapter has been omitted in our telling of the West at mid-century. Thankfully, Patricia Etter has taken a huge step in redressing that imbalance. This volume identifies, then thoughtfully evaluates, virtually every known source on the southern trails from the rush of 1849. Many have been published, usually in historical journals or by small presses; many others reside in archives from New Jersey to California. They document routes across the southwestern United States and some through Mexico to the California gold fields. Etter also includes works of that minority of later historians who wrote on the southern branch of the overland journey.

Here is a roundup of scattered testimony and history that provides for the first time the opportunity for the curious general reader to track down what is needed to learn about this neglected episode in the westward emigration of Euro-Americans. Anyone who wants to pursue this subject doggedly, perhaps to write a much-needed synthesis of the southern gold rush, will find invaluable guides to primary sources easily missed otherwise. In short, the way is finally opening for a redressing of a heretofore distorted story.

These accounts, for instance, show that the rush of 1849 was a truly national expansion. California-bound emigrants naturally followed lines of least resistance, typically moving westward as directly as possible and using the most accessible transportation. The Oregon-California trails, therefore, were taken mostly by pioneers from the Ohio River valley, the middle states of New York and Pennsylvania, and New England. Their voices have dominated the telling of the overland experience. But thousands of southerners also headed directly westward—in their case usually funneling through Fort Smith, Arkansas, or through Texas, then on through New Mexico and across the desert to southern California. The accounts laid out here by Etter are full of voices from Mississippi, Virginia, Tennessee, Arkansas, Texas, and other states of the

Atlantic and Gulf coastal South. By 1849 the societies of these states had grown so different from their northern neighbors that twelve years later the South would declare its independence. Like all overlanders, southerners carried with them attitudes of their mother societies, but Tennesseans and Alabamans had been reared culturally in their own ways. Their experiences and observations of emigration reflected a distinct regional view of the changing West, a perspective now more available because of this book.

Nearly everyone making the trip by whatever route was stunned by the encounter with country alien to all they had known before; but once again, these impressions have been presented almost wholly in the context of the central and northern plains. The southwestern deserts had their own boggling effect on those who crossed them. The meandering rivers that sometimes went to sand, the fantastic landscapes, the arid distances, and strange-looking plants all drew the attention of travelers, many of whom had come from the lush, humid South, where annual rainfalls were six to ten times that of the country they now faced. The shock of contrast, so common in the writing of emigration, was played out here in its own distinctive way.

The gold rush was also a social experience. People, often from varied backgrounds, were thrown together under trying conditions. They responded in diverse ways. Some cracked under the stress. Most weathered the passage, but none forgot it. The social tableau sometimes became high drama. One of the journals cited here, that of A. D. King, relates an extraordinary happening. Deep into the trip, an emigrant was knifed to death by a man he had taken in as a fellow traveler in his wagon. The company held a trial, convicted the attacker, then executed him by firing squad. Besides the story's pathos, it reveals how tightly these pioneers were holding on to social and legal forms as they moved westward. The detailed account of discussion, deliberations in the trial, and execution, a friend who is an attorney and legal historian tells me, show an attention and legal care as dense as in the documents on the trial and execution of Walter Raleigh.

To California on the Southern Route is a labor of love and of devotion. Patricia Etter has not only scoured archives across the country to bring together this bibliography: with her husband, Paul, she has also covered as much of the ground as possible in person, driving and hiking into mountains, through gullies, and over broken, rocky desert stretches. The result is an invaluable book on the gold rush and on the mid-century frontier. Like Merrill J. Mattes's *Platte River Road Narratives,* Etter's book is, in itself, a fine addition to an historian's shelf, and it is also a nearly irresistible invitation to pursue a neglected path into one of the most important stories of our western past.

ELLIOTT WEST

SAN MIGUEL DEL VADO CHURCH, 1805
*"Attended church today—Catholic, of course. The building is a large adobe
finished in the most rude style . . . the floor covered with rough boards upon
which all kneel, having no seats or benches"*
William Chamberlin 5:6/2. Author photo, 1988.

HISTORICAL OVERVIEW

When I started research on the Robert Brownlee journal, *American Odyssey (27)*, fifteen years ago, I encountered numerous difficulties trying to locate material dealing with migration on the Southern Route to the California gold fields during 1849. I did find hundreds of books dealing with every facet of the gold rush and the 35,000-40,000 argonauts who went west on northern trails. These diaries, with their editors' interpretations, have contributed to the study of the gold rush and its historical significance to the westward movement. By contrast, these same studies offer only a line or two about southern trails; many ignore them altogether. For example, J. D. Unruh alluded to the "so-called" southern trails in *The Plains Across* (1979), while George R. Stewart (*The California Trail*, 1962), Martin Ridge (*Atlas of American Frontiers*, 1993) and Clyde Milner II (*Oxford History of the American West*, 1994), made no reference to the existence of emigrant trails in New Mexico and Arizona. Finally, Merrill Mattes dismissed the Southern Route after noting that "there were trails by way of Arizona and northern Mexico but those who followed them were only a small fraction of the total number who went over land" (*Platte River Road Narratives*, 1988). The map illustrating his work shows a trail between Salt Lake City and Los Angeles, which he called "The Southern Route to California." Not so. That trail was the well-known Old Spanish Trail.

This neglect has not served history. Contrary to Mattes's statement, a significant number of goldseekers—some 20,000—trod southern trails to California in 1849. We must study that migration if we are to tell the whole story of the westward movement. For example, in 1987 Harlan Hague wrote that "if the whole story of the peopling of the West by overland travel is to be told . . . the story must *begin* with the southern route, because it was the first of the important overland trails in the American West" (*119* 1987:41). He went on to say that:

> Omission of the southern route from general accounts of the overland experience is due to the tendency of Americans, including historians, to view the unfolding of United States history as a movement westward from Jamestown and Plymouth. The term, 'colonial period,' in the popular mind means *British* America, the thirteen colonies . . . This view overlooks a *Spanish* colonial period in what is now the American Southwest which predated the British settlement, developed simultaneously, and lasted longer. The neglect of the region carries over to the Mexican and American periods as well (ibid., 50).

Lack of attention may also be due to the fact that the three major works dealing with the subject were published in limited numbers many years ago, so are absent from most library shelves. For example, Owen Coy's *The Great Trek (107)* came out in 1929; Ralph Bieber published *Southern Trails to California (100)* in 1937; and Grant Foreman followed with *Marcy and the Goldseekers (116)* in 1939. Nothing more appeared until 1970, when Ferol Egan wrote about the adventures of those who traveled across Mexico *(175)*. Finally, Harlan Hague's *The Road to California (119)* was published in 1978.

About twenty-five years ago, Glen Dawson and E. I. Edwards appended bibliographies to the Lorenzo Aldrich *Journal (14)* and *Lost Oasis Along the Carrizo (111)*. These comprised twenty-four reminiscences about Southern Route travel. This shortage of material surely led researchers to believe that few trod southern trails, hence there was nothing to be gained from further study. As a matter of fact, I was told that one scholar reportedly said: "The Southern Route? It has all been done."

My subsequent study of the newly collected material suggests that the Southern Route was more heavily used than previously thought. In addition, I found that historians have not agreed on consistent terminology when referring to trails by name, probably because there was not enough material to work with. To further confuse, emigrants often created their own names for sites. After analysis, I determined that the major trails within the Southern Route comprised the Gila Trail (upper and lower segments), the Southern Trail, and the shortcut, Apache Pass Trail. I also discovered that several adventurers on the list went to Zuni, New Mexico, then rode southwest to the junction of the Salt and Gila rivers near Phoenix, Arizona. Furthering the challenge, a few trod to the Yuma Crossing over the treacherous El Camino del Diablo (Devil's Highway) out of Sonora, Mexico.

This study also describes emigrant trails across Mexico and on the Baja peninsula. In addition, there were some important feeder trails that are located and described: the Santa Fe Trail; Fort Smith–Santa Fe Trail; and the Upper Emigrant and Lower Military roads in Texas. I will also critique the maps that accompany the published works in the bibliographic entries.

I have selected material from 1849 because it allows us to locate and study the original trail and move on to document the evolution of shortcut trails and others that led off toward new places. We learn that emigrants were not always blazing new trails in 1849. In the early days, the route was defined to take advantage of water sources on tracks laid out by the aboriginal population, which the Spanish, Mexicans, and mountain men had been using for centuries. A number of overland companies hired some of those mountain men—John Maxwell, John Hatcher, James Kirker—to lead them.

It is important to note that the trails did not always go east to west, but also from the south to north over the trade and migration routes long ago etched into the landscape by the Native Americans, Spanish, and Mexicans. This, of course, does not diminish the contribution of thousands of gutsy individuals who prodded weary and half-starved animals over every kind of terrain from lush forested elevations down to barren desert flats. It is not surprising to learn, therefore, that those who had had enough of California and overland journeys thought return by way of crowded boats and the steamy jungles of Nicaragua or Panama far less risky.

The bibliography lists and briefly describes the various trails and assigns a route code for each entry. It also describes the various feeder trails forty-niners used to reach one of the Southern Route trails. A section includes those travelers who led pack mules the full length of the Gila Trail, while another records the stories of those who joined the lower Gila Trail near the Pima villages after negotiating the Southern and/or Apache Pass trails. It is followed by a list of reference works about those trails. A final segment comprises those who risked travel across Mexico and/or the Baja peninsula, and is also followed by additional references. Each section is introduced with a historical survey of the trail. Annotations to each account highlight aspects of the trip from the diarist's point of view and include biographical information, when available, about the traveler.

We learn that these early immigrants had grit and were determined to seek adventure. Most were men. They were intelligent, creative, and well educated. A high percentage settled in California after briefly returning home for families. I made an interesting discovery as I studied these diaries. A number of writers "borrowed" varying amounts of material from the works of others and neglected to cite the source. John Russell Bartlett *(97)*, Josiah Gregg *(117)*, Randolph Marcy *(123)*, and William Hemsley Emory *(114)* were popular choices to quote from. Apparently, the concept of plagiarism was not a serious matter among overland travelers in the mid-1800s.

There are some fascinating characters represented here: a founder of the *San Francisco Alta California* newspaper; the founding fathers of both Sacramento and Oakland; a mayor of Sacramento; the future mother-in-law of John Muir; the collector of the Port of San Francisco; Abraham Lincoln's last appointee; judges and medical doctors; ranchers and vintners; treasurers and county clerks; individuals who participated in the 1851 Mariposa and Indian War; a famous actor; and one whose collection of Pleistocene vertebrates is today in the British Museum.

I scoured numerous catalogs, indexes, and on-line databases to locate manuscript material held in library collections throughout the United States. I am grateful to colleagues who supported my search and helped with material from their archives: Peter Blodgett at the Huntington Library; Bonnie Hardwick in the Bancroft Library; George Miles of the Beinecke Library; Daryl Morrison from University of the Pacific; and Eleanore Stewart with Stanford University Libraries. Harlan Hague, who has encouraged my studies of Southern Route migration for many years, read the manuscript and provided valuable suggestions for improvement. Others have assisted my on-site reconnaissance on the Southern and Gila trails. I will never forget the day Diana Hadley of Tucson helped hoist me onto a horse, then led me over the rugged Guadalupe Pass Trail.

Shelly Dudley, Salt River Project, Phoenix; Andrew Wallace, Northern Arizona University; and David Miller, Cameron State University, shared their expertise as I tried to define the route between Zuni Pueblo, New Mexico, and the junction of the Gila and Salt rivers. Delores McBroom at Humboldt State University, California, helped with information on Caspar Steinmets Ricks (80). No less important is the contribution of Rose Ann and Harland Tompkins, and Ruth and Jack Root, who expertly negotiated four-wheel-drive vehicles over bumpy roads, rocky hillsides, desert washes, and narrow canyons in search of elusive swales. Don Couchman of La Mesa, New Mexico, helped locate and interpret the Cooke's Pass area and guided us to long-lost Foster's Hole in New Mexico. Bill Cavaliere of Playas, New Mexico, was of enormous assistance introducing me to ranchers whose land the Southern Trail crossed. Harry Crosby of La Jolla, California, generously contributed the stunning photograph of a segment of the mission trail in Baja. Marcie Richie, a descendent of J. R. Forsyth, and Anne Perry, descendent of A. B. Clarke, generously offered photographs of their ancestors.

I must also acknowledge the Interlibrary Loan staff at Arizona State University, who energetically retrieved everything I requested. Lorraine Lineer of Sacramento provided invaluable research assistance. I am also grateful to Don Buck and the Oregon-California Trails Association, which has agreed to support work toward designating trails within the Southern Route a National Historic Trail. The Professional Development Committee for the University Libraries at Arizona State University awarded a generous grant to assist my research. I am grateful to friend and colleague Elliott West, who provided the foreword to this work, and to Bob Clark, who thought my efforts worth publication. Finally, I give special thanks to my husband, Paul, for his help in looking for trail segments, though he more than once wistfully mused: "it would be such fun if you were researching the Champagne grape."

Quotations from bibliographic citations use the number (in parentheses) followed by the date of diary entry or page number from the work quoted. Dates from diary entries do not include a year if they were written in 1849. I use date of entry whenever possible so readers will be able to consult the published version, a transcript, or holograph with equal ease. References cited from sources that do not appear in the annotated bibliography are placed in parentheses within the body of the text, e.g., last name of author or initials from title, year of publication, volume number if any, and pages cited. An alphabetical listing of those references follows the text. A glossary includes a description of people and places mentioned in the text or on maps that are not otherwise identified.

EXPLANATION OF ENTRIES

The various routes are detailed in each section. Sites that do not appear on modern highway maps are listed in the glossary with USGS coordinates. In addition, each journal entry is followed by two or three two-letter codes that show a feeder trail and the main trail that connected with it. For example, an argonaut who took the Fort Smith-Santa Fe Trail, moved along the Southern Trail to the Pima villages, and connected with the lower Gila Trail will have the following code: FS-ST-GT.

FEEDER TRAILS

FS The Fort Smith-Santa Fe Trail essentially followed the Canadian River. It passed Edward's Trading House at Little River, Antelope Mounds, a cluster of hills in a bend of the Canadian River, Oklahoma; crossed the Llano Estacado (Staked Plains) to San Miguel del Vado, New Mexico; then curved toward Pecos before terminating at Santa Fe.

SF There were two branches of the Santa Fe Trail between Independence and Santa Fe: the mountain branch went by Bent's Fort, Colorado; Raton Pass and Las Vegas, New Mexico; while the Cimarron Cutoff angled southwest from present-day Dodge City, Kansas, to Wagon Mound and joined the mountain branch near Las Vegas.

TT There were two main trails in west Texas: the Upper Emigrant Road advanced to Benjamin Franklin Coons's ranch (later El Paso) and El Paso del Norte (later Juarez) via Fredericksburg, Horsehead Crossing, and Guadalupe Pass in Texas; while the Lower or Military Road angled to Coons' Ranch by way of San Antonio and Comanche Springs (the site of future Fort Davis), then went north, paralleling the Rio Grande.

TM This code tells us that a traveler first trod one of the Texas trails to points along the Rio Grande, forded the river, and headed for the Guadalupe Pass trailhead on the Chihuahua–New Mexico border by way of Corralitos and Janos, Chihuahua.

PRIMARY TRAILS

GT   The Gila Trail ran the full course of the Gila River from New Mexico to its junction with the Colorado at Yuma. The portion between Truth or Consequences, New Mexico, and the Pima villages, Arizona, is the upper Gila Trail. The lower Gila Trail ran from the Pima villages to the Yuma Crossing on the Colorado. Travelers on the Southern Trail joined the lower Gila Trail at the Pima villages.

ST   Southbound travelers on El Camino Real out of Santa Fe or Galisteo joined the Southern Trail near tiny Garfield, New Mexico. I speculate that northbound travelers from El Paso also left the river near Garfield. The trail followed a southwesterly course toward Guadalupe Pass and Santa Cruz, Sonora, and continued north by way of Tucson to the Pima villages, where it joined the lower Gila Trail.

AP   The Apache Pass Trail went west from Soldier's Farewell Hill, New Mexico, to Tucson, Arizona, on a trail that snaked through a narrow defile between the Dos Cabezas and Chiricahua mountains.

MX   This designation includes trails and roads crossing Mexico from points along the Rio Grande or from Vera Cruz and Tampico.

SECONDARY ROUTES

BJ   The mission trail, El Camino Real, between Cabo San Lucas and San Diego, California, connected sites on the Baja peninsula.

BT   This designation includes those that sailed to San Diego or San Francisco out of San Blas or Mazatlán.

DH   El Camino del Diablo (Devil's Highway) was the primary route for Sonorans out of Mexico, which headed out of Caborca, Sonora, and angled northwest toward the Yuma Crossing by way of the hazardous Pinacate wilderness in southwestern Arizona.

ZU   This route went west from Albuquerque to Zuni, New Mexico, before turning to the southwest toward the junction of the Gila and Salt rivers west of Phoenix, Arizona.

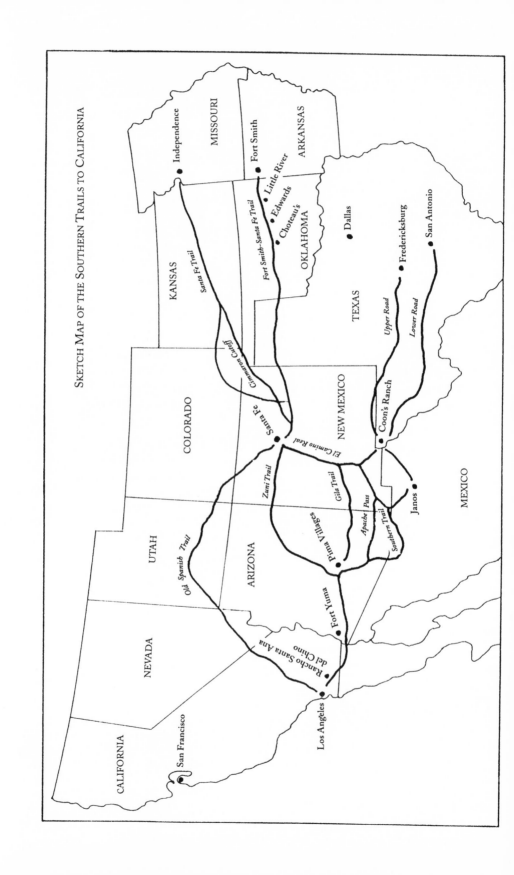

SKETCH MAP OF THE SOUTHERN TRAILS TO CALIFORNIA

WHICH WAY TO CALIFORNIA?

Though rumors had circulated for months, few took serious note until President Polk confirmed the news in his State of the Union message on December 5, 1848—there was indeed gold in California and plenty of it. Citizens all over the eastern United States were galvanized to action. Some 25,000 boarded ships to go by way of the Horn, or sailed to Panama, crossed the Isthmus, and caught another ship for San Francisco. Estimates vary, but it is reasonable to say that from 35,000 to 40,000 adventurers traveled overland from Independence or St. Joseph, Missouri, to start a journey on the northern route by way of the Little Blue and Platte rivers.

Independence was also the jump-off point for the well-worn Santa Fe Trail, which had sustained an active trade since 1821. A number of travelers, impatient with the wait at Independence, learned they could travel to Santa Fe and connect with either the Gila or Southern trails to California. Twenty diarists left vivid stories about that trip. Some set a course along the mountain branch of the Santa Fe Trail, which went to Bent's Fort in Colorado then entered northern New Mexico by way of Raton Pass. Scores of travelers avoided the Rocky Mountains by taking the Cimarron Cutoff, a waterless *jornada* which angled southwest (near modern Dodge City), passing Wagon Mound, a prominent natural feature and landmark northeast of Santa Fe. In the early days, caravans were required to register at San Miguel del Vado, a community dating to the 1790s, which was for many years the port of entry for

RATON PASS, NEW MEXICO.
"Some time today we passed through fine Pine Groves which threw out a grateful shade.
At other times over rough uneven Rocks but take it all together this crossing of
the Ratone Mountains was by no means so difficult as was anticipated"
John Robert Forsyth *48*:7/27.
Photograph courtesy of National Archives, 30N 618 0 Box 22F West #38.

New Mexico. After that, they were allowed to continue toward Pecos Pueblo and, finally, roll into the longed-for destination, the city of Santa Fe.

At least one argonaut on the Santa Fe Trail was enchanted by the Rockies. On July 3, John R. Forsyth woke to a fine morning and found the

> Sun bright and beautiful. Still reclining in this romantic country & viewing nature in her native grandure—unassisted by the puny Efforts of man. Here she puts on the most Magnificent dress every thing on a

scale of Grandeur. Extended Plains. Elevated Mountains. Rocky
Precipices deep Ravines, filled with immense Pines. The beautiful
Planes extending from the feet of the Mountains covered with rich
grasses *(48)*.

While travelers on the Santa Fe Trail were admiring the Rockies, thousands of Arkansans and residents from other southern
states strained the facilities at Fort Smith, Arkansas, where they
prepared to head for Santa Fe along the Canadian River. Creative
entrepreneurs in Fort Smith began promoting the reopening of a
trace that Josiah Gregg had blazed in the spring of 1839 on which
he had moved a large caravan of goods for trade in Santa Fe. As a
matter of fact, his book *Commerce of the Prairies (117)*, a classic in
its own time, was available to the prospective goldseeker. It was
filled with advice for the traveler and included colorful descriptions
of the various New Mexican towns and their inhabitants.

The thousands of emigrants that gathered in Van Buren and
neighboring Fort Smith, Arkansas, would not be traveling unpro-
tected. Arkansas senator Solon Borland petitioned the secretary of
war to provide a hundred-man military escort for the forty-niners.
At the same time, it would survey the route for a national road to
California. Captain Randolph B. Marcy, graduate of the U.S. Military Academy and veteran of the Mexican War, was chosen to
command the escort. It struck out from Fort Smith on April 4,
1849. Marcy's report, including a fine historic account of the trip to
Santa Fe, is told in Grant Foreman's *Marcy and the Goldseekers*
(116).

There are some thirty-two reminiscences that recount the trip
between Fort Smith and Santa Fe, and, for most, it was a grand
adventure. Almost as soon as they left Fort Smith, the travelers
were in Indian Territory (Oklahoma), which had been set aside for
the Five Civilized Tribes, who had been forcibly removed from
their homes in the southern states: Chickasaw, Choctaw, Creek,
Seminole, and Cherokee. The first major stop was Little River,
about 125 miles from Fort Smith. Arriving on May 31, George

Sniffen recalled his delight at meeting and shaking hands with Wild Cat, the colorful war chief of the Seminoles: "A stalwart noble looking man about 6-1/2 feet in height and dressed in a beautiful Indian costume, brilliant with silver ornaments, beads and cloth" *(84)*. Others never forgot James Edwards, who for many years was the patriarch of a Creek settlement near Little River, and whose trading post became a popular rendezvous for the emigrants. Here William Goulding went native. He purchased seven tanned deer skins and engaged one of Edwards's daughters to make an "Indian costume . . . after the most approved native style" on April 6, 1849 *(51)*. Moving down the road to Choteau's Fort a few weeks later, William Chamberlin spent some time on May 3 examining and measuring the ruins of the trading post belonging to frontier trader and Indian diplomat August Pierre Choteau. It had been slowly falling to ruin since his death in 1838 *(5)*. Though it would seem that travelers should have been anxious to get to California, individuals like Chamberlin often took time out to go sightseeing, climb a mountain, or measure a ruin.

The travelers marveled at the fat prairie dogs. As a matter of fact, Robert Brownlee found them "good eating" (*27*:58). However, all this paled beside the most anticipated adventure on the plains, the buffalo hunt. Stanislaus Lasselle was awed on April 29, when he said he saw thousands of the animals "as far as the eye could reach." He watched the men make a number of chases, more for the sport than the meat, since the woolly beasts were hard to shoot. When they did cook a kill, most found the meat leathery and hard to chew *(12)*. "Oh cracky!" lamented Arkansan John Boyer, "In vain our grinders brought to bear on it; its toughness was a quality that absorbed all others; it was abandoned" (*Arkansas State Democrat*, 9/7/1849).

The forty-niners stayed close to the Canadian River as far as modern Tucumcari, New Mexico. On May 6, William Goulding crossed the famed Llano Estacado (Staked Plains) and came face to face with a friendly Comanche chief who rode into camp on his

The Seminole, Coacoochee (Wild Cat)
"He is a stalwart noble looking man
about 6-½ feet in height and dressed in
a beautiful Indian costume, brilliant
with silver ornaments, beads and cloth."
George S. Sniffen *84*:5/31.
Courtesy, The Florida State Archives

Coacoochee, (Wild Cat.)

mule. He described him as having "a most jovial and excellent disposition." He went on to say that the chief was covered in yellow
body paint with his hair braided around a strip of buffalo hide and
silver plates that reached almost to the ground. A necklace of bone
beads, a belt of silver, many bracelets, and buffalo hide wrapped
around part of his body completed the picture *(51)*. Stanislaus Lasselle was looking on that day and noted that the chief was invited to
breakfast. There was no knife or fork, and Lasselle said the Indian
let them know by signs that he was well acquainted with the use of
those utensils *(12)*.

On entering the village of San Miguel on May 25, David Jordan
commented that the adobe town looked like a "large Brick yard."
Then he fell in with custom and attended services in the fifty-year-

Comanche Indian, who *"appeared to be a most jovial and excellent disposition."* William Goulding 51:5/6. Courtesy, Yale Collection of Western Americana, Beinecke Rare Book and Manuscript Library.

old Catholic church before dancing away the rest of the day at a fandango *(64)*. "The way the native population waltzes is a caution to cripples," said one correspondent to the *Arkansas State Democrat* (8/17/1849).

The Santa Fe and the Fort Smith–Santa Fe trails merged near Las Vegas and San Miguel del Vado before passing the extensive Anasazi ruins of Pecos Pueblo, which had been constructed some 400 years earlier. When John Forsyth arrived on August 8, he marveled at the height of the crumbling buildings. He noticed that the

PECOS PUEBLO, NEW MEXICO.
"At night a few of the men explored the ruins with torches & dup up a part of the floor which was found full of Human bones. One of the Mummys was in perfect state of preservation. Money was the object of the digging but none was found"
John Robert Forsyth *48*:8/8. Author photo, 1988.

carved roof of the adobe church still retained its ornaments. In addition, he watched a number of men excavate some house floors by torchlight. They were crestfallen when they found human bones instead of money or other treasure *(48)*.

Oh, how they anticipated the exotic color of old Santa Fe! Most were disappointed. Some described a great mud city surrounded by sandy soil and scrubby cedars. Others found the prices too high. Then there were those who disapproved of gambling, especially the card game monte, which was almost a national sport. Nor did they adjust to the fact that many women smoked. On another level,

William Chamberlin admitted to being moved as he approached Santa Fe on June 7 and saw the "Stars and Stripes floating in the breeze." He was also attracted by a sign advertising the comforts of the U.S. Hotel. With visions of a soft, clean bed, a hot bath, and some good food, he hastened forth only to find he was to be housed with thirty others in "a small uncleansed stable, infested with fleas, bedbugs and other vermin, the stench being horrible" *(5)*.

Others entered the spirit of the thing and learned to play monte or dance an energetic fandango or two. And if they happened by on June 24, St. John's Day, they had the opportunity to watch *Correr el Gallo*, which Josiah Gregg thought to be "one of the most attractive sports of the rancheros and the peasantry, and that which more than any other calls for the exercise of skill and dexterity." He went on to describe the sport in more detail:

> A common cock or hen is tied by the feet to some swinging limb of a tree, so as to be barely within the reach of a man on horseback; or the fowl is buried alive in a small pit in the ground leaving only the head above the surface. In either case, the racers, passing at full speed, grapple the head of the fowl, which being well greased, generally slips out of their fingers. As soon as some one, more dexterous than the rest, has succeeded in tearing it loose, he clasps spurs to his steed, and endeavors to escape with the prize. He is hotly pursued, however, by the whole sporting crew, and the first who overtakes him tries to get possession of the fowl, when a strife ensues, during which the poor chicken is torn into atoms. Should the holder of the trophy be able to outstrip his pursuers, he carries it to a crowd of fair spectators and presents it to his mistress, who takes it to the fandango which usually follows, as a testimony of the prowess of her lover (*117*:241–242).

Most travelers bypassed the Santa Fe road and followed a track to the hamlet of Galisteo, which had been colonized by Hispanic settlers during Mexican rule. John Robert Forsyth visited the alcalde on August 10 and said he "was much pleased with his kindness. His house was well furnished, having a clock & some other American furniture. His lady was a fat comly Dame & set us down some excellent Brandy & Wine and cut Glass tumblers" *(48)*.

Adobe ruin in La Joya de Seviletta, a few hundred yards from the Rio Grande with the Ladrón mountains to the west, "*is another brick-yard looking place, containing some 250 inhabitants*"—William W. Hunter 62:8/14. Author photo, 1996.

Another resident in the friendly village introduced Judge Benjamin Hayes to the tortilla, which he ate with relish when he stopped by on October 19 *(54)*.

The argonauts continued southwest toward the Rio Grande, passing long-abandoned Anasazi pueblos near Abo and Quarai and their imposing mission ruins. The road angled toward the centuries-old village La Joya de Sevilleta, where forty-niners found apples and sheep for sale. In the early days, this was a staging area for southbound wagons on El Camino Real. Moving along the east side of the river, they would pass the hamlets of La Joyita and Sabinal before fording the river to Socorro. A number of travelers crossed the Rio Grande at Albuquerque and moved downriver on a branch of El Camino Real past Isleta Pueblo and the towns of Belen, Polvadera, and Lemitar before arriving in Socorro. At Socorro, they started to think about the next leg of their journey: whether to join the Gila Trail or the Southern Trail.

But first, let us guide some forty-niners to Coons' Ranch and El Paso del Norte over Texas roads. About 33 percent of Southern Route overlanders sailed from East Coast ports or New Orleans to Galveston, Port Lavaca, or Corpus Christi, where they began to assemble with companies of Texans also planning the great trek. We learn from the accounts that the Texas sojourn was tedious and often dangerous. This was because there were barely any roads or settlements west of Fredericksburg in 1849. In addition, there was the ever-present anxiety about meeting up with hostile bands of Comanche or Lipan Apache Indians.

Those who decided to take the Upper Emigrant Road needed to make their way to Fredericksburg, a German settlement of some 300 souls and the last outpost of civilization. Coons' Ranch would be 600 weary miles away. The ranch, on the east bank of the Rio Grande, would become El Paso in 1858. El Paso del Norte, across the river in Chihuahua, would later be known as Juarez. Travelers primarily followed a route laid down by Major Robert S. Neighbors and John S. Ford, who had set out in March 1849 to find the most practical way to the town. As a matter of fact, Robert Beeching writes about meeting the two men May 29 on their return to San Antonio *(21)*. The trail went northwest by way of the San Saba, Colorado, and Pecos rivers; climbed over Texas's Guadalupe Mountains; and dipped down to a watering hole at Hueco Tanks before going on to Coons' Ranch.

Travel on the Lower or Military Road sorely tried Thomas B. Eastland's patience. He traveled with John Coffee Hays *(55)* and his engineers while they surveyed the new road. On September 11 he wrote that it took "*Ninety-seven days*, of irksome delays and travel . . . distance according to my own *daily* estimates, 693 miles, over a trackless, and hitherto unexplored wilderness, following in the wake of an Army, whose slow movements were made slower still by the engineers and Road Makers . . ." *(146)*. Eastland ultimately went across Mexico to Mazatlán, where he found passage to San Francisco.

In the meantime, most of the new arrivals at Coons' Ranch or in El Paso del Norte journeyed to a spot where they could take the Southern Trail. A number went north along the Rio Grande for about eighty miles and joined the trail near San Diego Mound or Garfield. Others dropped into Mexico and followed a road by Corralitos and Janos to the Guadalupe Pass trailhead near the international border with New Mexico. L. N. Weed took the first choice after an interview with the alcalde of El Paso del Norte. He was told that the laws of Mexico would not let them bring in coffee and bacon and any found with such goods in tow would be thrown into prison. Since Weed admitted that coffee and bacon were his principal provisions, he opted to go north to San Diego Mound, which he did on June 9 *(91)*.

San Diego Mound is a prominent feature forming the east bank of the Rio Grande thus forcing travelers to a narrow trail on the opposite bank. Author photo, 1996.

Those who went by Corralitos and Janos toward the southern entrance to Guadalupe Pass had to keep a sharp eye since the area was often under siege by the Apaches. As a matter of fact, Benjamin Butler Harris tells of meeting the Apache leader Mangas Coloradas in Janos, who assured him that "he loved Americans" (52:70). At the same time, Mangas was wary because a number of emigrants, lured by the prospect of making a quick buck, went into the Apache-hunting business after the governments of Sonora, Chihuahua, and Durango sponsored bounty programs paying $150 for the capture of each live Apache woman and child under fourteen and $250 for a live warrior or $200 for his scalp (Smith 1964:17).

Most folks on the so-called feeder trails got along fairly well. There were hardly any skirmishes with Indians (more individuals were hurt or killed with their own guns); cholera disappeared as they moved inland; water, wood, and feed for animals were generally available; the animals were not yet trail worn; and they could all refresh and recruit in numerous New Mexican villages. But there would be hard times ahead as they entered the western desert, where water was the most prized possession.

FORTY-NINERS ON THE GILA TRAIL

INTRODUCTION

The Gila Trail had long been known to Indians, Spaniards, Mexicans, and mountain men and ran the full length of the Gila River to its junction with the Colorado at Yuma. The upper half was a rugged pack trail which connected a point near modern Truth or Consequences, New Mexico, and the Pima villages in Arizona. Because of this, it was not heavily traveled in 1849; I estimate that fewer than 500 plodded the course. There are thirteen reminiscent accounts, including one forgery. In contrast to what one might expect, the travelers kept bumping into people in the vast forested expanse. Apache Indians appeared from time to time, hoping to trade mescal for other goods, and there was the odd courier carrying mail between California and Santa Fe, according to Joseph Simmons, who met one on August 12 *(83)*.

The Gila Trail began its westward climb out of the Rio Grande valley in the vicinity of Truth or Consequences, and meandered through what later became the Gila National Forest. Gaining altitude, a traveler could look back to catch some exceptionally fine panoramic views of the New Mexico terrain. A convenient rendezvous and jumping-off spot was the Santa Rita del Cobre copper mines near modern Silver City, New Mexico. These began production in the 1800s to supply the Spanish royal mint in Mexico City but were abandoned around 1834 due to Apache incursion.

General Stephen Watts Kearny, guided by Kit Carson, led his Army of the West along this route in 1846 as he made his way to

California. His chief astronomer, Lieutenant William Hemsley Emory, published his classic report of the trip in 1848, and we learn that numerous forty-niners pocketed a copy of his *Notes of a Military Reconnaissance* to help them negotiate the rugged trail *(114)*. There are two recorded attempts to retrace the trail. With the encouragement of Senator Carl Hayden of Arizona, the War Department issued orders in 1937 for army engineers to retrace the route between Santa Fe and Yuma. They were to select points where the route of the Army of the West coincided with modern highways (Carl Hayden Papers). In 1957 George Ruhlen went on site to complete a reconnaissance of that trail between the Rio Grande and Silver City and published the results of his study in the *New Mexico Historical Review (130)*.

On leaving the copper mines, goldseekers and their pack animals headed for Night Creek, later renamed Mangas Springs, honoring the meeting between Kearny and the Apache leader Mangas Coloradas, who promised friendship to Americans (the site is thirty miles west of Silver City, New Mexico, near milepost 94 on U.S. Route 180). Emigrants followed Night Creek to its junction with the Gila River, which they followed all the way to the Pima villages. There is hardly a place where the emigrants could set their course in a straight line since that river meanders around mountains and through valleys on its way to the Colorado. A modern-day pathfinder can view the Gila terrain at Red Rock at the end of New Mexico 464 or visit the farming community of Virden off New Mexico 70, both north of Lordsburg. At Duncan, on the Arizona–New Mexico border, the Gila takes a sharp turn north, cutting through canyons of solid rock, thus forcing riders to high ground. Lieutenant Emory named this canyon the "Devil's Turnpike" in 1846, as did emigrants who wrote about it in their diaries. On Thursday, July 12, 1849, William Chamberlin wrote that he was at the point where he had to leave the river to cross the "Turnpike." He said that "here the mountains close in upon the river, which has cut a channel through solid rock, in places more than

100 feet high. Through these cañons its restless waters rush, making it impossible to continue our course down the river. We drove our stock to the top of the mountain to feed . . ." Travel had not improved by Friday the thirteenth, when their "course was over mountains and through ravines, down the rocky beds of which we frequently traveled for miles. Our mules scrambled along the sides of mountains and precipices where I thought it would be impossible for man or beast to venture . . . the trail for the whole distance is covered with sharp stones, which severely lacerated the hoofs of our animals . . . " (5). The Devil's Turnpike terminated at the confluence of Bonita Creek and the Gila River near Safford, Arizona. A monument commemorating Emory and Kearny's 1846 encampment was later erected on the site.

One group risked travel down the bed of the river. On July 12, Stanislaus Lasselle related the saga of a comrade, David Buchanan, who was accidentally shot in the thigh. Since the doctor could not extract the bullet, the others fabricated a litter from willow poles and carried him up and down mountainsides, and then along the river to the Pima villages, where they arrived on July 23 (12).

Here, the tired travelers rested and exchanged tales of adventure with argonauts coming off the Southern Trail, which terminated at the villages. William Chamberlin straggled in on July 26. He wrote that he met a Captain Day and his wife, the first female emigrant he had seen on the route: "she was mounted upon a mule, riding in the train covered with dust, holding an umbrella over her head and a child in her arms" (5).

Wagons could now roll along the lower Gila Trail from this point to the Yuma Crossing on the Colorado River. But before moving on, forty-niners traded with friendly Pima farmers, loading up on supplies of the American triumvirate, corn, beans, and squash. Emory heaped praise on this peaceful group for its generosity and honesty. These Indians had no use for money but traded willingly. According to John Durivage, the Pima had "an extraordinary partiality for shirts of all colors, and in fact it is the only current coin in the place"

(*42*:219). Alden Woodruff of the Little Rock Company complained that almost every wagon lost some articles while encamped and added "that they might have been honest when Lt. Emory was among them, but they have learnt bad manners since" (*Arkansas State Gazette & Democrat*, 4/26/1850).

Both wagons and pack trains moved along the lower Gila toward its junction with the Colorado at Yuma. Coming up was a tough push over a 40-mile desert that cut across a 160-mile bend in the Gila River. Summer temperatures often topped 110 degrees so travelers tried to move at night. Dry, alkali dust was everywhere. Cacti native to the Sonoran desert crowded the trail, so both animals and men tried to avoid contact with needle-sharp spines. Forty-niners had survival to think about, but a section of this route between Mobile and Gila Bend preserves one of the most pristine and beautiful segments of the Sonoran desert. It was later named Butterfield Pass.

A site on the south side of the Gila River, about fifteen miles west of Gila Bend, was known as Murderer's Camp when a cattle drover, Richard Dallam, passed by in 1853. He correctly repeated the murder story had that played itself out back in 1849 (1852–1864:58). It did not take long for the real facts of the case to be twisted into legend. In 1858 Waterman Ormsby wrote that the name derived from a murder committed in 1856 by a wealthy young man who shot and killed his guardian in a fit of passion. Emigrants who witnessed the crime executed him on the spot and buried him next to his victim (*128:* 99–100). The event took place on September 5, 1849, and is described in Alfred D. King's diary *(65)* and confirmed in at least ten other emigrant diaries. It was also referred to on September 30 in Isaac Williams's "Rancho Santa Ana del Chino Register Book" *(102)*. Robert Beeching reached the spot on September 20, where he "found written in ink on a large sheet of paper the history of a very melancholy occurance wich took place..." *(21)*.

We learn that a generous-hearted Elijah Davis of Arkansas had offered to board and support the less-affluent George Hickey on the California journey. They had a disagreement on the day in question and exchanged harsh words. According to witnesses, Hickey made the first threatening move with his knife. Davis was unable to dodge the attack and died almost immediately after Hickey stabbed him. The men of the Clarksville (Arkansas) Company empaneled a jury, put Hickey on trial, and found him guilty. The jury recommended a military-type execution. Twelve guns were to be loaded—six with powder and ball, six with powder only. Twelve men drew lots to be on the firing squad, then selected rifles at random so they would not know who had the loaded weapons.

The grave had been dug near Davis's last resting spot. Hickey was put in the grave while the Reverend Mr. Gwin delivered a prayer and the firing squad took position. "Ready, aim, fire!" Hickey fell back as several balls hit him square in the chest. In 1995 the site was covered by dense brush; there is nothing to recall the drama that played itself out in September 1849.

Because of repeated flooding over the years, many miles of the lower Gila Trail are silted over and not visible. However, Painted Rocks State Park, west of Gila Bend, Arizona, preserves one of the most outstanding collections of petroglyphs in the Southwest. Numerous forty-niners camped here and commented about the "hieroglyphics" that Lieutenant William Emory sketched in his report. A few miles down the road at Sears Point is Independence Rock, where over the years travelers had etched their names in the desert varnish. John W. Jackson of the New York Knickerbockers stopped to carve his name before moving on. John L. Hatcher, guiding James Collier, also scratched his name for posterity. A traveler with a four-wheel drive and a map from the Bureau of Land Management in Yuma, Arizona, can visit this location by leaving Interstate 8 and driving north on Spot Road to Sears Point.

Forty-niners on southern trails had few problems dealing with the various American Indian tribes they met along the way. Most learned, however, that they could expect trouble dealing with the Yuma Indians, who challenged their patience as they attempted to

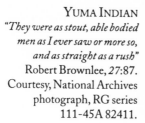

YUMA INDIAN
*"They were as stout, able bodied
men as I ever saw or more so,
and as straight as a rush"*
Robert Brownlee, 27:87.
Courtesy, National Archives
photograph, RG series
111-45A 82411.

cross the Colorado to California. Frederick J. Thibault of the Little Rock Company called them the "pests of the Colorado" who showed "cool audacity and cunning" as they thought up creative ways to relieve forty-niners of their possessions *(90)*. Since there was no ferry at the Colorado crossing in 1849, emigrants counted on the fine Yuma swimmers to tow their belongings across the river. But as time went on, these Indians became so hostile that the U.S. Army sent Lieutenant Cave Couts to the area to protect the emigrants *(106)*.

The Gila Trail ends at Yuma, Arizona. Some California-bound emigrants crossed the Colorado River near its confluence with the Gila, while others moved downstream some ten miles to a point known as Pilot Knob. There was a third crossing a few miles below Pilot Knob. For many, the crossing signified arrival in the golden land and the end of their journey. Dr. David Jordan arrived at the river on August 3 and reported that as soon as William Goulding

H. M. T. Powell sketched Yuma Crossing at the junction of the Gila and Colorado rivers
in 1849. *"I ascended the rocks which here form the ramparts of the Rio Colorado they are about
100 feet high and the view was extended and beautiful. The distant Mountains presenting
every outline that it was possible for rugged, piked, precipitous, broken mountains to assume."*
J. R. Forsyth 8:11/7. Courtesy, the Bancroft Library.

of the Knickerbocker Company saw the running water "he fired off
his double-barreled shot gun & cried out at the top of his voice '*Oh!
praise the Lord all ye pack mule men for having brought you safe through
the desert,*' then he took off his hat and gave 3 cheers ..." *(64)*.

Once across the Colorado, the trail dipped into Mexico to avoid
the drifting sands of the Algodones Dunes. It passed Cooke's Well
(near Paredones, Baja) and Second Well (Alamo Mocho, Baja)
before swinging north passing modern Calexico and New River.
From this point, much of the trail is preserved in Anza Borrego
Desert State Park. Rangers there have carefully researched and

Viewpoint on Campbell Grade, Anza-Borrego Desert State Park looking south to Vallecito Valley with the old wagon trail clearly visible.
Author photo, 1984.

marked existing segments of the emigrant road, which they have named the Southern Emigrant Trail. Visitors will have no trouble retracing the steps of the forty-niners to Warner's Ranch. At the ranch, many emigrants decided to go to San Diego and find water passage to San Francisco, while others made up their minds to continue on foot to the mines. The following group of thirteen diaries represents the record of the minority that trod both the upper and lower portions of the Gila Trail.

FORTY-NINERS ON THE GILA TRAIL

SOURCES

1. ANONYMOUS

   "Rough Abstract of a Forty-Niner's Diary." Typescript (February 3, 1849–August 24, 1852) in the Bancroft Library.

   Here is a 5-page abstract of a 322-page diary that is packed with details and dates. This appears to be a shortened version of the Phineas Blunt diary (3) since the dates of diary entry are an exact match. Like Blunt, he went to work as a police officer since he failed as a miner. [FS-GT]

2. BLAIR, CHARLES M.

   Memorabilia of Charles M. Blair with an Account of His Duel With Colonel Kasey, by Charles M. Wallace the Younger. Richmond, Va.: n.p., 1942. The rare pamphlet can be found in the California State Library, Bio Info File.

   This account is far from satisfactory since the author merely lists points passed on the way to California. Blair started out from Richmond, Virginia, and traveled across Louisiana and Texas to Coons' Ranch, where he turned north along the Rio Grande to the Gila Trail junction. He joined the New York Knickerbockers somewhere along the line since he signed in with them at the Rancho Santa Ana del Chino on September 6, 1849. Blair won the duel, by the way. [TT-GT]

3. BLUNT, PHINEAS UNDERWOOD, 1809–1897

   "Notes of Travel From New York to the Gold Region of California in the Year Eighteen–Hundred and Forty-Nine, February 5, 1849–January 14, 1852." Manuscript and typescript (1849–1852) in the Bancroft Library.

Blunt recalls his trip with the New York Knickerbockers. The 322-page diary contains detailed and carefully composed descriptions of a number of sites including Pecos Pueblo, New Mexico, and of a day in the life of a New Mexican and of the Pima villagers in Arizona. He observed more drama than most. He saw a Mexican shot for stealing mules; a slave killed for refusing to accompany his new owner; and described the scene at San Miguel Mission in California, where the William Reed family had been brutally murdered (Browne 1950: 64-67). Since the manuscript is so detailed, it is excellent for studying the route of the upper Gila Trail and the trials and privations emigrants suffered as they negotiated the vast wilderness.

Phineas Underwood Blunt.
San Francisco *Call* 1/16/1897.

They lost their way a number of times and had good reason to be grateful that Apaches were on peaceful terms with American travelers in 1849, since those Indians directed them to water sources and the right trail.

Blunt arrived at the Rancho Santa Ana del Chino on September 14, 1849, then headed for the Feather River, where he prospected for a short time before joining the San Francisco police force. Ultimately, the New Hampshire native spent twenty-two years with San Francisco's custom house and made money on the side from real estate ventures. [FS-GT]

4.   BROCKWAY, H. S.

Across the Southern Trail to California. Mount Pleasant, Mich.: John Cumming, 1982. Reprinted from the *Jonesville (Mich.) Telegraph*, May 9, 1850.

The twelve-page booklet contains two letters that Brockway wrote to his children. He left La Grange, Fayette County, Texas, on April 4, 1849, and appears to have followed the Upper Road by way of the Guadalupe Mountains in Texas to Coons' Ranch. In his first letter, written at Doña Ana, New Mexico, on June 9, he said that he was planning to strike west on Kearny's old trail (the Gila Trail). This was an unusual decision since all emigrants of whom we have record followed the Southern Trail if they were heading north from Coons' Ranch or El Paso del Norte. The second letter describes the vicissitudes of travel along the Gila River and notes his safe arrival in California. There is no hint in the small book about his fate. [TT-GT]

5.   CHAMBERLIN, WILLIAM H.

"From Lewisburg to California in 1849," edited by Lansing C. Bloom. *New Mexico Historical Review* 22 (1945): 14–57; 144–180; 239–268, 336–357. This originally appeared in the *Lewisburg (Penn.) Saturday News,* between August 1902 and January 1903.

The extensive, well-written journal, one of the best to date, minutely recounts the journey between Fort Smith and Santa Fe, and the pack trip along the full course of the Gila River. Chamberlin left Fort Smith on March 28, 1849, and documented his daily activities including sights and scenes along the way. In addition, he listed weather and road conditions and added comments about his companions. He was plagued by homesickness on the Fourth of July and wistfully reminisced: "Instead of listening to a patriotic oration, or joining in a picnic on the green amidst the fair forms and sweet smiles of the dear girls, the incessant 'huppah mulah' is ringing in our ears as we plod along over the barren waste, or wend our way up and down the rocky heights." Two of Chamberlin's mess, Robert B. Green *(8)* and David Howard *(10),* also wrote journals that have survived. [FS-GT]

6.   D. H.

"Overland Route to the Pacific, Washington, Jan. 19." *New York People,* January 27, 1849.

This letter appeared in a rare newspaper and is included mainly to alert researchers that some reports are not always what they seem. For example, the trail described here is the Gila Trail, and the only extant description at this point in time was contained in William Hemsley Emory's *Notes of a Military Reconnaissance (114),* which was published in 1848 and certainly not available in time for someone to take the trail and return to the United States to write about it. Moreover, a good deal of the descriptive material, including latitudes and longitudes, is paraphrased directly from Emory. [-GT]

7.   ELIOT, ROBERT, 1830–1917

"A March Letter: Off to the Gold Fields with Robert Eliot," edited by Lillian Krueger. *Wisconsin Magazine of History* 30

(March 1950):327–340. The letters are also found as "Account of Journey," *Essex County (N.Y.) Republican,* March 16, 23, and 30, 1899. There is a typescript in the Wisconsin Historical Society Collections.

Eliot and members of the Albany Company journeyed by way of the Fort Smith–Santa Fe Trail and were on the road by April 18, 1849. After reaching Albuquerque, the men moved south down the Rio Grande, then turned west to the Gila Trail at modern Truth or Consequences. On July 2 he wrote about his meeting with the Apache leader Mangas Coloradas, who in addition to having "very courteous manners," proudly showed off defective rifles with upward-curved barrels. Eliot said that trappers deliberately sold them to the Indians supposing they would not know how to adjust the aim in order to hit a target.

The writer offers an interesting account of his activities in the mining region, including Mariposa, Sacramento, and Nevada City. After two years' sojourn in California, Eliot moved to Milwaukee, where he became a partner in one of the largest companies in the old Northwest dealing in grain commodities. No doubt he entertained his partners from time to time with vignettes from his western travels. [FS-GT]

8.   GREEN, ROBERT B., 1821–1849

On the Arkansas Route to California in 1849. The Journal of Robert B. Green of Lewisburg, Pennsylvania, edited by J. Orin Oliphant. Lewisburg, Pa.: Bucknell University Press, 1944.

Green traveled with William H. Chamberlin *(5)* and David Howard *(10)*, and his diary supplements those two works nicely. Green was generous with his comments and criticism of his comrades, the incompetency of army officers, and his opinion of the Indians. The *Alta California* reported his untimely death on January 9, 1850, noting that he was interred by the Davy Crockett Masonic Lodge. [FS-GT]

9.   HAMMOND, JOHN, 1827-1889

John Hammond: Died May 28, 1889, at His Home, Crown Point, NY. Chicago: P. F. Pettibone, 1890. Copies are in the Bancroft and Newberry libraries. Also in the Bancroft is *Overland to California* (microform) by General John Hammond, [1899?].

Hammond was leader of the Albany Company. A colleague, Robert Eliot, his "brother clerk," also left reminiscences of the trip *(7)*. After purchasing the company's outfit in New York and shipping it around the Horn, Hammond went to Van Buren, Arkansas, to join his companions. His overland experience is contained on pages 40–45, where we learn that the men supplied themselves with rubber boots, suits, caps, gloves, cups, canteens, and even a rubber boat. He tried mining at a number of locations, including Nevada City, before returning to his business in Crown Point, New York, in April 1851. [FS-GT]

10. HOWARD, DAVID "DEACON"

"Journal of David Howard." Transcript (1849) in the Ellen Clark Bertrand Library, Bucknell University.

Howard's journal complements those of Robert Green *(8)* and William Chamberlin *(5)*, two of his traveling companions. [FS-GT]

11. HOYT, JOHN P., 1817–?

"Mr. John Hoyt's Notes and Account of His Travels." Dictation in William R. Goulding's "Journal" *(51*:266–280). Manuscript (1849) in the Yale Collection of Western Americana, Beinecke Rare Book and Manuscript Library.

Hoyt stayed with the Knickerbocker Company as far as Santa Fe, where he broke off with the main contingent in order to take the Old Spanish Trail to Salt Lake by way of Abiquiú in the Chama River valley of New Mexico. This was an unusual decision since use of the trail had declined considerably; the last recorded travel had been in 1848. Hoyt describes how they coped with dreadful weather, narrow escapes from flood waters, and the sudden truancy of their guide. Thus the men retraced their steps and completed their journey on the Gila Trail. Hoyt arrived at the Rancho Santa Ana del Chino on August 21, 1849, where he became reacquainted with William Goulding *(51)*, who copied Hoyt's dictation into his own diary. [FS-GT]

12. LASSELLE, STANISLAUS, 1811–1852

"The 1849 Diary of Stanislaus Lasselle," edited by Patricia A. Etter. *Overland Journal* 9, no. 2 (1991):2–33. A truncated version was published by Dunbar H. Seymour in *A History of Travel in America*, Appendix M. New York: Tudor Publishing Company, 1937. Original manuscript is in the Charles B. Lasselle Papers, Indiana State Library; a typescript is in the Huntington Library.

Lasselle and nineteen companions started for Fort Smith from Logansport, Indiana, on February 6, 1849. The fact that he was a lawyer and publisher of the *Logansport (Ind.) Canal Telegraph* may account for his ability to record detailed notes, including vignettes about Indians, missionaries, and traders he met along the way. Lasselle's participation in the Mexican War no doubt influenced his decision to travel a southern route and also hardened him for the rigors of the journey. As a matter of fact, he often poked fun at his greenhorn traveling companions as he recalled each day's events. On April 28 he noted that a "Knickerbocker was boiling all of the coloring out of his shirt"; on April 30 he wrote that "a Knickerbocker lost a horse in chasing a Buffalo"; on May 7 he said "a Knickerbocker shot a bear after it was dead"; and on May 11 he saw "a Knickerbocker kicked by a mule." He continued to detail his trip in this manner until his arrival at the Rancho Santa Ana del Chino on August 21.

Lasselle enjoyed some success in California, since records show that he sent $2,162.32 by Adams Express to the Philadelphia Mint. He died soon after his return to Logansport. [FS-GT]

13. TAYLOR, JOSEPH [FORGERY BY WILLIAM G. UNDERBRINK]

A Journal of the Route from Fort Smith, Ark. to Calif. in the year 1849. With a full account of the trail, necessary equipment, and many other interesting facts as experienced on route. Bowling Green, Mo.: Job Office, 1850. Reproduced on microfilm no. 5488. New Haven, Conn.: Research Publications, Inc., 1975. (Western Americana, Frontier History of the Trans-Mississippi West, 1550–1900.) Referenced in the Everett D. Graff Catalog (1968), no. 4084.

Everett Graff offers an interesting account of his purchase and discovery of this fraud and includes his correspondence with Edward E. Eberstadt, also reproduced in the microfilm edition. The fifteen-page publication was thought to have been based on the Stanislaus Lasselle diary in the Indiana State Library. There were six copies of the clever forgery; three were destroyed. One copy was given to the New York Public Library and is contained in its collection of frauds and forgeries.

FORTY-NINERS ON SOUTHERN TRAILS

INTRODUCTION

The Southern, Apache Pass, El Camino del Diablo, and Zuni–Salt River trails are discussed in this section. The Southern Trail lured by far the greatest number of emigrants, and there are some sixty-two diaries and reminiscences from which to study the adventure. This trail left the Rio Grande near Garfield, New Mexico, fifteen miles north of the landmark, San Diego Mound. Philip St. George Cooke *(104)* was credited with taking the first wagons over this road when he led the Mormon Battalion to California in 1846. The first point of interest was Foster's Hole, a natural cistern enclosed by a hundred-foot volcanic wall some fifteen miles west of the Rio Grande. Its location was lonely and forgotten until 1994, when members of the Southwest Chapter, Oregon-California Trails Association (OCTA) located and mapped the site.

Cooke's Springs and Pass in Luna County, New Mexico, provided a good rest spot. Historic use of this abundant water resource began about 1780, when Juan Bautista de Anza visited the spring. Since then, thousands have sipped its good water, including members of the Mormon Battalion, emigrants of 1849, and travelers on the Butterfield Stage. Later, the Atchison Topeka & Santa Fe Railroad diverted the water to a tank some four miles away, which continues to supply local needs.

The pass curves between two low hills before it opens out to magnificent views of the Mimbres Valley and the changing form of

Massacre Peak at every turn of the road. Sadly, this was the last stopping point for a number of travelers. In one rare case, emigrants took time out to bury a comrade and carve an inscription on a rock headstone. Southwest OCTA members noted and mapped the feature in 1995. It remembered J. Chaffin of Platte County, Missouri, who died on November 21, 1849. Coincidentally, Judge Benjamin Hayes described Chaffin's illness, last days, and sad burial in his diary *(54)*. The next stop was on the Mimbres River, where D. Lambert Fouts found "a splendid spring, the water was cold and perfectly clear as cristal" (*49*: July 23).

Emigrants were entering Apache country and in 1849 found those Indians very friendly and anxious to trade mules for a variety of presents. Moving on to Ojo de Vaca (Cow Springs), travelers came on the road connecting Janos, Chihuahua, with the copper mines near modern Silver City. We learn from diaries that some went off on a fruitless search for gold before giving up and moving south toward the picturesque Coyote Hills. It was here that I was able to identify Vista Tank as "the watering spot for fifty animals," which Lieutenant Emory sketched on his map *(114)*. After winding through the hills for ten miles or so, travelers emerged to a panoramic view of the Animas Mountains with Playas Lake appearing as a shimmering streak along the base. Usually dry, the lake bed provided a hard surface for wagons to cross before rolling over Whitmire Pass into the lush Animas Valley.

Heading for the Guadalupe Pass trailhead near the international border, emigrants might meet travelers who had taken the El Paso-Janos road, one of the so-called feeder trails. Here they commenced travel over Guadalupe Pass. There is no easy "pass" through the Guadalupe Mountains, as I found in 1983. Instead, my horse stayed on a trail that followed contours close to the summits, most over 5,000 feet in elevation. After several steep ascents and descents, the trail makes a winding but gradual descent to the northwest before entering Guadalupe Canyon. I photographed the

Looking southeast to trail leading out of Guadalupe Pass, New Mexico.
"We came to the brink of a descent, that would make the head swim to look down.
This our wagons had to descend probably 800 or 1000 feet in half a mile, and to pass
over the ground one would pronounce it for wagons impassible."
F. J. Thibault *90*:8/1. Author photo, 1982.

Guadalupe Pass Trail meanders southwest toward Guadalupe Canyon.
"When I came abruptly to the brink of this frowning gulf, it was a sight that caused me
to pause and gaze with admiring awe on a scene of black and terrible desolation....
Well might the boys say, 'we have overtaken the elephant at last.'"
F. J. Thibault *90*:8/1. Author photo, 1982.

spot where forty-niners were compelled to rope wagons down a 1,000-foot descent and where Frederick J. Thibault noted that "one miss drive, and a wagon whirled to destruction" and "where no one felt inclined to trust himself on the back of his animal for fear of performing a somerset over its head. To take a seat on the verge of this descent, and view this mountainous and broken landscape, would fill the beholder with dread" (*90:* 7/11/1851).

The trail enters Guadalupe Canyon and follows a meandering

stream. On September 15, William Hunter *(62)* found "some of the most wild and rugged scenery imaginable. At every turn of the Creek, some new feature was presented tending to add grandeur or sublimity to the vista, while the beautiful green canopy above shielded us from the rays of the sun. . ." Hunter spoke the truth; Guadalupe Canyon is a most beautiful place. Exiting the canyon, emigrants moved on to the San Bernardino Rancho, abandoned in 1837 by its owner, Lieutenant Ignacio Perez, due to incessant Apache raids. Descendants of the old San Bernardino herd, now wild, roamed the area and provided sport and food for emigrants.

Some travelers were treated to a fandango at Santa Cruz, Sonora, where they were also able to purchase home-grown peaches and apples. Times were not good in the small Mexican village on September 26, when Benjamin Stevens *(85)* came into town. He reported that Apache Indians had recently driven off residents' cattle and horses and that no man left his house without a sharp spear attached to the end of a ten-foot ash pole. On leaving the village, travelers marched north along the lovely Santa Cruz River valley passing the mission, Tumacacori, and the presidio of Tubac. Apaches were also giving the Papago (Tohono O'odhan) tribe near San Xavier del Bac mission plenty of trouble, and when John Robert Forsyth arrived on October 4, he found the Papagos celebrating a successful battle against the Apaches by performing a dance around a pole from which their trophies—two bloody scalps—were suspended *(48)*.

The trip from Tucson to the Pima villages could be reasonably pleasant or sheer hell. It all depended on the time of year. July was a sizzler. On the eleventh David Jordan described how they set three buckets of water by the side of the road, and as travelers came in, "they rushed to them & drank like maniacs." He told how one man "jumped right into the river & laid down & opened his mouth & let the water run in" *(64)*. The Southern Trail terminated at the Pima villages, and it was here that travelers rested up before risking travel on the forty-mile desert in order to bypass a bend in the Gila River. From that point, wagons could roll along to the Yuma Crossing.

The Apache Pass Trail, opened almost by accident, ultimately became Interstate 10, one of the busiest routes in Arizona. There are five reminiscent accounts of travel on the route in 1849: John Caperton *(30)*; David Durie Demarest *(41)*; Robert Eccleston *(45)*; John Coffee Hays *(55)*; and John Nugent *(71)*. On October 14 Hays and members of his company stopped to rest near Soldier's Farewell Hill, some miles west of Deming, New Mexico. By chance, they met General José María Elías, who was commanding a punitive expedition against the Apaches. David Demarest wrote that Hays asked the general if there was a more direct route to Tucson instead of the road by Guadalupe Pass. The general said it could be done and left two guides to help them on their way.

Apache Pass, also known as Puerto del Dado, is a narrow defile between the Dos Cabezas and Chiricahua mountains in southeastern Arizona. For some years following 1849, it was frightening and dangerous for travelers since Apache Indians found the terrain ideal for ambush. In 1849, however, Robert Eccleston described the scene as "a romantic one. We followed the bed of a dry arroya where there was scarcely room for the wagon wheels, let alone room for the driver. This road was overshadowed by handsome trees, among which I noticed the pecan, the ash, oak, willow, &c." *(45:*184). The route covered some 200 miles, passing Willcox Playa and the Galiuro and Little Dragoon mountains, then crossing the San Pedro River before continuing west to Tucson.

A close study of the William Brisbane *(26)* and Edward Griffin Beckwith *(20)* diaries led to discovery of a route between Zuni Pueblo and the junction of the Salt and Gila rivers a few miles west of Phoenix, Arizona. Beckwith was with Captain Herman Thorn's dragoons, assigned to accompany James Collier *(33)* to California to take up his post as collector of the Port of San Francisco.

Andrew Randall *(79)* was also a member of this small company. They were guided by John L. Hatcher, who had frequently trapped the area.

As far as can be determined, the route went southwest from Zuni to Silver Creek (near Snowflake, Arizona), and past Clay and Deer springs on the Mogollan Rim. It left the Rim at Carrizo Creek, moved south to follow the Salt River, passed its junction with both Tonto Creek and the Verde River, then came on the ruins of a Hohokam village (later known as Pueblo Grande in Phoenix) before arriving at the Gila River. The men were challenged by exceedingly rugged terrain, "Alps on Alps and nothing but Alps," William Brisbane moaned on September 17 *(26)*. When Grant Foreman wrote the story of James Collier's trip to California *(33)*, he would have welcomed the Brisbane *(26)* and Beckwith *(20)* diaries, which minutely outlined the trip. He was not able to define Collier's route with accuracy since he worked with the scanty amount of material available at the time.

The last trail of concern is El Camino del Diablo, sometimes called hell on earth. Three individuals in this list may have followed the trail to the Yuma Crossing: Job Francis Dye *(44)*, James Hobbs *(57)*, and Cal Hubbard *(58)*. However, there is no doubt that this was the favored route of thousands of Sonorans on their way to the gold fields. Starting at Caborca, Sonora, the 250-mile trip to Yuma covered sere desert flats and shoe-ripping lava malpais over what was known as the Pinacate wilderness. Summer temperatures soared to 120 degrees and stayed there. Travelers counted on replenishing water supplies from natural rock basins such as Tule Tanks and Tinajas Altas. If Tule Tanks was dry, and it often was, a traveler was challenged to make it to the next source of water at Tinajas Altas. If those tanks were dry, travelers simply died of thirst. A multitude of graves at the site are a grim reminder about the danger of summer travel in the desert without adequate supplies of water.

ROBERT BROWNLEE. See item 27.
History of Solano County, San Francisco, 1879

ASA BEMENT CLARKE. See item 32.
Courtesy, Ann Perry.

JOHN ROBERT FORSYTH. See item 48.
Courtesy Marcia W. Richie.

O.M. WOZENCRAFT. See item 95.
*Ingersoll's Century Annals of San
Bernardino County, 1904:686.*

FORTY-NINERS ON SOUTHERN TRAILS

SOURCES

14. ALDRICH, LORENZO D., 1819–1851

A Journal of the Overland Route to California and the Gold Mines, edited by Glen Dawson. Los Angeles: Dawson's Book Shop, 1950. Reprint of the Lansingburgh, N. Y., (1851) edition in the Huntington Library.

Aldrich left New York on April 18, 1849, and headed for Fort Smith, where he joined the migration to Santa Fe. He followed the Southern Trail, arriving safely in San Diego on December 3. He faithfully recorded each day's events, which included detailed descriptions of the road and the assorted companies and individuals he met along the trail. Aldrich, like many men on the trip, had to learn to cook. For the most part, they were proud of their efforts. He went hunting on August 19, shot some wild fowl—partridges, curlews, and brants—and put them into some "glorious pot-pies." We learn that he went to the northern California mining camp of Rough and Ready and stayed until the following November, when he left for home by way of Panama. Sadly, the young man died from an illness contracted on the Isthmus just two weeks after reaching home.

Dawson included a reprint of Robert Creuzbaur's 1849 map "The Gulf of Mexico and the Mississippi Valley to California and the Pacific Ocean" *(108)* that illustrated the various trails as he perceived them. [FS-ST-GT]

15. ANONYMOUS

"East Bank of the Colorado River, Nine miles below the mouth of the Gila, State of Sonora, Mexico, November 22, 1848," *New Orleans Picayune,* July 11, 1849.

This short, descriptive letter is included here because it gives the first evidence that parties set out for California before President Polk's December 1848 confirmation of gold discovery in California. The 115-wagon outfit left Camargo, Mexico, on July 16, moved on through Chihuahua, and probably joined the Southern Trail at Guadalupe Pass. [TM-ST-GT]

16.   ANONYMOUS

"From Texas to the Gold Mines," edited by Ralph P. Bieber. *Southern Trails to California in 1849*, vol. 5, Southwest Historical Series. Glendale, Calif.: The Arthur H. Clark Company, 1937. Pp. 260–280. Also found as "Sketches from the Journal of a Traveler, Overland to California." *La Grange Texas Monument*, February 19, 26, and March 5, 12, 1851.

The nameless pioneer pulled out of Austin, Texas, on April 8, 1849. He and his companions appear to have taken the Upper Emigrant Road to Coons' Ranch, although he is often vague about locations. They journeyed through Corralitos and Janos in the Mexican state of Chihuahua, then rode north to join the Guadalupe Pass road where it connected with the Southern Trail. His daily notes briefly describe the terrain and camp sites, the availability of water and wood, and number of miles traveled. Unlike many who abandoned their diaries on arrival at the Yuma Crossing, this traveler continued his entries until he arrived at the southern mines on September 5, 1849, when he wrote: "The diggings of Mariposa were before us! Our journey was ended!" [TM-ST-GT]

17.   ANONYMOUS

Walking on Gold, by Phyllis Crawford. New York: Julian Messner, Inc., 1940.

Crawford created a fictional account of the overland journey from a fragment of an uncle's letter. The hero of the tale was a delightful Scotsman, who pushed his wheelbarrow for 2,500 miles along the Fort Smith–Santa Fe and Southern trails. As a result, he suffered little since he had no animals to feed and water or wagons to repair. The author portrays the route accurately.

18.   AUDUBON, JOHN WOODHOUSE, 1812–1862

Audubon's Western Journal: 1849–1850. Being the MS record of a trip from New York to Texas, and an overland journey through

Mexico to Arizona to the gold-fields of California, edited by Frank Heywood Hodder. Cleveland: The Arthur H. Clark Company, 1906. The University of Arizona Press released a photographic reproduction of the first edition in 1984.

Audubon was the son of naturalist John James Audubon. He leaves a memorable saga of adventure resulting from a combination of bad luck and ill-considered decisions. Thirteen comrades died of cholera near Rio Grande City, Texas; a major part of a $27,000 bankroll was stolen; there were problems with supplies; and finally, a significant number of men turned tail and went home. The remainder pushed on with little food and minimal survival skills on a rarely used route.

Instead of taking the trail to Guadalupe Pass, the group traveled along the Chihuahua road as far as Parral, then struck across a killer mountain track to Altar, Sonora. Turning north toward Arizona, they trudged over Papago (Tohono O'odham) territory toward the Pima villages on the Gila River. Here they joined the emigrant trail and struggled toward the Colorado as best they could. Cornelius Cox wrote that he met Audubon on October 11 near the Yuma Crossing: "the first instance of distress I had seen on the road—Many of these men had not a days provisions on hand—and some were entirely destitute" *(36)*.

In spite of adversity, Audubon not only managed to produce a number of sketches but kept up daily diary entries that provide valuable ethnographic material and descriptions of the flora and fauna. Thirty-four of his drawings are sheltered in the Southwest Museum in Los Angeles. The rest were lost in transport when the steamer *Central America* sank. The Audubon drawings are reproduced in *The Drawings of John Woodhouse Audubon: Illustrating His Adventures through Mexico and California, 1849–1850* (Book Club of California, 1957). Audubon had arrived home earlier to fulfill numerous family responsibilities, which combined with many anxieties, were thought to contribute to his early death. The diary of Jacob Henry Bachman *(19)* should be read in conjunction with the Audubon journal. [MX-GT]

19.   BACHMAN, JACOB HENRY, 1815–1879

"Audubon's Ill-Fated Western Journey," edited by Jeanne Skinner Van Nostrand. *California Historical Society Quarterly*, 21(1942):289–310. "Diary of a 'Used-up' Miner," edited by Jeanne Skinner Van Nostrand. *California Historical Society Quarterly* 22 (1943):67–83.

Bachman was John Audubon's cousin and spells out the reasons their 240-day journey to Eldorado was filled with more disasters than most. The second journal contains sketchy entries, which cover his experiences and life in the mines to 1878, shortly before he died. [MX-GT]

20.   BECKWITH, EDWARD GRIFFIN, 1818-1879

Journal, August 22–October 6, 1849. Manuscript in the Huntington Library.

Lieutenant Beckwith was serving with the detachment of dragoons led by Captain Herman Thorn, which was assigned to escort James Collier, the newly appointed collector for the Port of San Francisco. The dragoons joined Collier and his company in Santa Fe in late August. With John L. Hatcher as guide, they set a course for Zuni, arriving on September 5. Hatcher led the travelers along one of his old trapping routes toward the junction of the Salt and Gila rivers, which they reached on September 29. William Brisbane's daily trip record *(26)* is a very close parallel to Beckwith's daily notes.

Taken together, the observations of the two men have been a great help in defining a strenuous journey over some of the most rugged terrain in Arizona. Even with Hatcher as a guide, it is a wonder that these travelers made it to their destination. On the September 17 Beckwith wrote that they "were often without a trail—no one knows our whereabouts but the only mountain man with us thinks we are on or near the Salt River." Beckwith assumed leadership of the dragoons after Thorn drowned at the Yuma Crossing. He retired as major, 2nd U. S. Artillery, in 1879. [SF-ZU-GT]

21.   BEECHING, ROBERT, 1814-1894

"Journal of a Trip From New York on the Bark Norumbega to Galveston and thence Overland through Texas, Mexico, Arizona, and Southern California to San Diego 1849, March 8–October 20." Manuscript in the Huntington Library.

Beeching began his great adventure with the P. F. Smith Company from New York in company with two diarists listed here, David D. Demarest *(41)* and L. N. Weed *(91)*. This group directed its course over Texas's Upper Emigrant Road to Coons' Ranch. Beeching tells about meeting Major Robert S. Neighbors, who was returning to San Antonio after surveying that road. He regularly records the vicissitudes of summer travel over the parched plains of northern Texas. While in camp on June

24, some of the men began making an American flag from red silk hand-kerchiefs and blue shirts in anticipation of a celebration on the Fourth of July, which Beeching said they would use—if they were still alive. He writes frequently about missing his family and friends but keeps his faith throughout. On September 11, as he approached the end of his journey, he repeated his philosophy: "so I'll praise God for all that is past and trust Him for all that's to come." Thus he persevered and made it safely to San Francisco, where David Demarest found him on January 21, 1850, run-ning a tent store "selling coffee, cakes and pork and beans" *(41)*.

Soon after, Beeching opened a blacksmith shop. He took part in local activities, including the vigilance committee and the prison commission, where he earned the title, "Prisoner's Friend" (*San Francisco Call* 10/23/1894). We also learn that he was a good Methodist, who was ordained a deacon of the First Church in Alameda, California, some time in 1873 (Anthony 1901:338). [TT-ST-GT]

22.   BIRT, SAMUEL P., ?–1859

"The Journal of the La Grange Company . . ." Refer to the La Grange Company *(67)* for complete bibliographic cita-tion and description of the route.

Birt was one of three diarists who recorded entries in the journal. The company started out on Texas's Upper Emigrant Road and then followed the Southern Trail. Birt's contribution ceased on September 3, near the Yuma Crossing, when he left the company for reasons unknown.

We have few details on Birt's early life. He arrived in Texas about 1836, fought in the Mexican War, and left his wife and family in Texas when he came to California in 1849. It is not known if he ever went back to Texas, though he still owned property there at the time of his death in California (*67*: 196). [TT-ST-GT]

23.   BOULDIN, JAMES E.

"Diary of Captain James E. Bouldin—1849–50." Typescript in the Department of Special Collections, Stanford Univer-sity Libraries.

From information within the diary, we learn that Bouldin left Glas-gow, Missouri, on May 30, 1849, and traveled with Colonel Congreave Jackson's train of 200 men. The first part of the diary is missing; this por-tion begins on September 4, while the group was encamped in the Mim-bres River valley "where we had the most beautiful scenery to behold that ever men witnessed." Bouldin wrote that though the trip was tedious at times, he enjoyed himself. He kept a daily record of mileage and sites, and paid particular attention to description of the flora and fauna. This diarist writes about the Howard family, who tried to move down the lower Gila on a flat-bottomed boat. He was present on October 27 when Mrs. Howard gave birth to the first American child born in Arizona. Bouldin said, "let it be male or female its name shall be Gila..." Unlike many who stopped writing after reaching the Yuma Crossing, Bouldin continued describing his trip to the Mariposa mines. He included descriptions of many of the declining California missions as he moved along. He made his last entry on February 20, 1850. [SF-ST-GT]

24.   BOYLES, JOHN R., ca. 1834–1860

"None Dream But of Success," edited by Sarah N. Shouse. *Tennessee Historical Quarterly* 26 (1977):512–523.

Here is a badly edited article that reproduces segments of letters held in the Eliza H. Ball Gordon Papers in the Perkins Library, Duke University. It adds little to our knowledge of the overland experience. Boyles's letters to his mother—seventeen of them—are available for study, however. Written between March 13, 1849 and August 1850, they contain a good deal more gossip about the folks back home than facts about the journey. We do learn that Major Robert Farquharson led the company out of Fayetteville, Lincoln County, Tennessee. This company has been variously called the Lincoln, Fayetteville, and/or Tennessee company in a number of emigrant diaries. [FS-ST-GT]

25.   BRAINARD, DAVID

"David Brainard's Journal, Delaware, March 20, 1849– November 29, 1849." Manuscript (1849) in the Bancroft Library; typescript in the State Historical Society of Wisconsin.

Brainard recorded the travels of the Walworth Mutual Mining Company (New York) and included lively vignettes about his experience on the Santa Fe and Southern trails. He was especially fascinated by New Mexican life and culture, and like many other Americans, considered himself superior. On July 17 he wrote that Santa Fe "has the appearance of a dilapidated brick kiln" adding that "a more degraded class of human beings I never saw. Gambling is their principal employment. Every hotel is filled with men, women and children, Betting at the Monte tables." In addition to his colorful comments about his traveling companions, Brainard's diary is a good source for study of the trail.

Brainard chose the Isthmus route in 1851, when he returned to Delevan, New York, with a considerable amount of money. Restless, he hired on as cook and bookkeeper in various logging camps. On a day in midwinter, he disappeared from camp. Some time later, his friends found him frozen to death in a deserted shack. [SF-ST-GT]

26. BRISBANE, WILLIAM, 1823–1880

"Journal of a Trip, or Notes of One, from Fort Leavenworth to San Francisco via Santa Fe, in 1849." Manuscript in the Princeton University Library. There is a typescript in the Huntington Library.

As mentioned in the Beckwith citation *(20),* Grant Foreman wrote his *Adventures of James Collier (33)* with the few documents available in 1937. The addition of Brisbane's account has been a valuable help in defining the route. Foreman did clear up one mystery—the reason for Brisbane's presence in the group. It appears that Collier recruited thirty young men to serve in customs houses after their arrival in California *(33:*13). Brisbane complained about the food, which was mainly coffee and flapjacks if they had anything at all. He also tired of Collier's leadership but apparently tried to keep peace with the man since he expected to be working for him in California.

Brisbane was present when Captain Herman Thorn drowned in the Colorado on October 16. He wrote that Thorn's canoe capsized and he "was drowned by a Mexican clinging to him—every exertion was made to save him but poor fellow, he sank to rise no more . . . it has cast more gloom over us than starvation could." He added that Lieutenant Edward G. Beckwith *(20)* took command of the escort.

In a foreword to the manuscript, Brisbane's granddaughter wrote that he received an honorary degree from Princeton University in 1854, then went on to study homeopathic medicine at the University of Pennsylvania. He practiced in Wilkes-Barre until called to service during the Civil War and mustered out a brigadier general. In 1872 he served as U.S. consul to Ghent. [SF-ZU-GT]

27. BROWNLEE, ROBERT, 1813–1897

An American Odyssey. The Autobiography of a 19th-Century Scotsman, Robert Brownlee, at the Request of his Children.

Napa County, California, October 1892, edited by Patricia A. Etter. Fayetteville: University of Arkansas Press, 1986. A truncated, unedited version of Brownlee's memoirs appears in *Publication of the Society of California Pioneers* (1947): 11–36. Typescript copies are in the Bancroft Library and Arkansas Territorial Restoration, Little Rock.

Robert Brownlee, a stone mason, emigrated to America in 1837 and found work cutting stone for the state houses of North Carolina and Arkansas. When gold fever struck, he joined the Little Rock Company and left for California in April 1849. Though he writes about events many years after the fact, his recollections are accurate. His book also makes good reading since he was a fine storyteller.

The editor went on site to locate, map, and photograph sites mentioned in the autobiography. Endnotes recreate the trip over Playas Lake, Guadalupe Pass, and other major landmarks on the Southern Trail. A biographical list of known travelers out of Arkansas is included. Brownlee also provides anecdotes about life in the mining camp of Agua Fria, California, and concludes with an account of his pioneer ranching experience in the Napa Valley. [FS-ST-GT]

28. CAMERON, JOHN B., 1814–?

"Journal." Manuscript in the Department of Special Collections, Manuscripts Division, Stanford University Libraries.

Cameron was the last of the trio of diarists who contributed to the "Journal of the La Grange Company," which was published in the *Quarterly of the Tuolumne County Historical Society* in 1966 *(67).* The holograph manuscript, written in one hand and attributed to Cameron, appears to be a copy of the original document.

Cameron's contribution is quite colorful since he spelled his words phonetically. He took his leadership position seriously and worked hard to document the journey between the Colorado Crossing and the southern mining district. For example, on September 5 the party decided to travel at night to avoid the intense heat in the Colorado Desert. Cameron describes the journey thus: "our travel to knight is duemagnetic west over a deep sand road, boutyfull moonlight knight no vegitation nothing cold be seen but shining sand banks, thus we marched silantley threw the stillness of the knight, nothing to meete our eres but the gingling of the chaines . . ." Cameron guided his company safely to Sullivan's Creek, where they arrived on November 10, 1849.

Cameron ultimately went into the general merchandising business in Sonora, invested in real estate, and had some mining claims. In 1855 he formed a partnership with William H. Rulofson to produce daguerreotypes. He also pioneered a new route over the mountains between Sonora and Bridgeport (67:219). The 1863 *Directory of Nevada Territory* lists him as a resident of Aurora. [TT-ST-GT]

29. CANDEE, J. G., 1804–?

"Extracts From a Letter From Dr. J. G. Candee, late of Harwinton, to Anson Hungerford, Esq." *Hartford (Conn.) Courant,* September 14, 1850. A copy of the document is in the Bancroft Library.

Candee, a widower who said he lived at 20 Park Place, New York (CKEC), joined the New York Knickerbockers and headed for California on the Fort Smith–Santa Fe Trail. We learn about dissension in the group and how half split off to try their luck packing along the full length of the Gila River. Candee opted to stay on the Southern Trail. He wrote that he arrived in California with a change of socks and enough meat for one meal. There is no further record of his activities. [FS-ST-GT]

30. CAPERTON, JOHN

"Life and Adventures of John C. Hays, the Texas Ranger." Manuscript (1879) in the Bancroft Library.

The reminiscences were recorded by Hubert Howe Bancroft from material provided by Major John Caperton and Colonel John Coffee Hays *(55),* who escorted a group of emigrants to California in 1849. The trip was noteworthy because the men charted a new cutoff for Tucson, the Apache Pass Trail. The David Demarest *(41),* and Robert Eccleston *(45)* accounts provide the best details of the trip. [TT-AP-GT]

31. CHATHAM, J. W.

"Overland Journey, February 27, 1849." Manuscript in the Special Collections Library, University of New Mexico, Albuquerque.

Chatham offers an interesting account of his trip across Alabama,

Mississippi, and Tennessee, en route to Independence, Missouri, his departure point for California. He connected with the Southern Trail in Santa Fe. The 182-page diary ends at Quarai, New Mexico. In addition to facts about his trek, Chatham leaves us with a recipe for curing malaria and a list of rocks he collected along the way. Chatham makes a brief statement about Hezekiah J. Crumpton *(38)*, who traveled close by. Chatham said he came from Cambridge, North Carolina. [SF-]

32. CLARKE, ASA BEMENT, 1817–1882

Travels in Mexico and California, edited by Anne M. Perry. College Station: Texas A&M University Press, 1988. *Travels in Mexico and California: Comprising a Journal of a Tour from Brazos Santiago, through Central Mexico by way of Monterrey, Chihuahua, the Country of the Apaches, and the River Gila, to the Mining Districts of California.* Boston: Wright and Hasty's Steam Press, 1852.

Clarke joined the Hampden Mining Company of New York, leaving for California on January 29, 1849. He arrived at Brazos Santiago, an island near the mouth of the Rio Grande, and followed roads through the state of Chihuahua toward the southern trailhead at Guadalupe Pass. His plans were delayed, for a while at least, since he suffered from a painful swollen knee and was unable to travel for many weeks. Clarke recalls the saga of his forced confinement in the alcalde's house in Janos, where neither he nor his host spoke the other's language. Eventually, he recovered and joined another California-bound group. In spite of this delay, he could still be counted among the early arrivals, for he was busy in the mines by July 30, 1849. Clarke's book is particularly valuable for studying the Mexican portion of the journey. The author's map is reasonably accurate, though some places are misspelled.

We learn that he spent time in both Marysville and Sacramento, where he sold supplies to the miners before returning to his native Massachusetts in 1851. He married Margaret Hedges in Westfield that year and went to law school. Then in 1854, he moved to Independence, Iowa, where he bought a farm, dabbled in real estate, and ran a drug and grocery store. [MX-ST-GT]

33. COLLIER, JAMES, 1789–1873

The Adventures of James Collier, First Collector of the Port of San Francisco, by Grant Foreman. Chicago: Black Cat Press, 1937.

Grant Foreman used the only material at hand in 1937—excerpts from Collier's letters along with newspaper reports and official correspondence—in an attempt to reconstruct the overland trip. Collier was not a goldseeker but was on his way to California to assume the post of collector at the Port of San Francisco. He quit Fort Leavenworth, Kansas, on May 17, 1849, but was held up in Santa Fe until August laying in supplies.

Collier was a hot-headed leader whose patience had run thin by September 19, as his party came off the Mogollan Rim. We learn from William Brisbane *(26)* that Collier struck and kicked a member of the company, and Captain Herman Thorn of the dragoon escort considered putting him under arrest. As noted in the introduction, I have reconstructed the probable route using the Brisbane and Beckwith *(20)* diaries, topographic maps, and some on-site reconnaissance, with advice from colleagues. Amiel Weeks Whipple's 1853–1854 map *(134)* is a help in defining the route, though it is not entirely accurate.

Collier arrived in San Diego on November 1. He pursued his duties as first collector with great difficulty, and it was not long before controversy and numerous enemies forced him from his post early in 1851. He returned to Steubenville, Ohio, where he served as president of the Citizen's Bank. [SF-ZU-GT]

34. CONWAY, MARY, 1832–?

"Little Rock Girl Rides on Horseback to California in Gold Rush Days." *Pulaski County Historical Review* 12 (1964):6–9. Also published in the magazine section of the *Little Rock Arkansas Democrat*, September 22, 1963.

Mary Conway, along with her parents and nine brothers and sisters, left Fort Smith, Arkansas on April 11, 1849, close on the heels of the military escort provided by Captain Randolph B. Marcy. Much of the story can be followed in Grant Foreman's *Marcy and the Goldseekers (116)*. The short article mainly centers on the romance that developed between young Mary and one of Marcy's lieutenants, M. P. Harrison, who was killed by Indians on his return to Arkansas. A number of people were enchanted by the love story, including Cave Couts *(106)*, who spent a pleasant time with the family at the Colorado Crossing on October 28. In time, Mary wed sea captain Robert S. Haley *(116*:338). [FS-ST-GT]

35. COUNTS, GEORGE, 1805–1898

"A Journal of the Travel of George Counts to California in

1849." Typescript in the Arizona Historical Society, Tucson. The George Counts Papers, 1849, containing copies of diary,(March 23–May 4, 1849), travel agreement, and miscellaneous papers are in the Bancroft Library.

Counts, a Missouri native, left his legislative post in Clinton, Arkansas, and joined the Clarksville Company for the trip to California. His daily account of camp sites and miles traveled out of Fort Smith ends in Stockton on November 30, 1849. He noted his arrival in the "Register" at the Rancho Santa Ana del Chino on October 16, 1849 *(102)*. Count's journal was copied from the original by Richard Obar on July 22, 1900, near Coulterville, California.

Malinda Tong, Count's wife, eventually joined her husband in Mariposa County, California, where she helped earn a living by sewing. He held public office as Mariposa County treasurer (CSL). [FS-ST-GT]

36.   COX, CORNELIUS C., 1825–?

"From Texas to California in 1849," edited by Mabelle Eppard Martin. *Southwestern Historical Quarterly* 29 (1925–1926): 36–50; 128–146; 201–223. The Huntington Library houses Cox's "Notes and Memoranda of an Overland Trip from Texas to California in the Year 1849"; a photostat from the original is in the Ayer Collection, Newberry Library, Chicago. For notes about his later life and a reminiscent account of his journey, see "Reminiscences of C. C. Cox." *Texas Historical Association Quarterly* 6 (October 1902):113–138, and 6 (January 1903):204–235.

Cox left Harrisburg, Texas, on April 14, 1849, and after adding his name to the "Register" at the Rancho Santa Ana del Chino on November 7 *(102)*, pushed on to Stockton, California. This adventurer chose travel on Texas's Upper Emigrant Road to Coons' Ranch, where he turned north on the Rio Grande toward the Southern Trail junction near modern Garfield, New Mexico. Then Cox and fellow members of the Harrisburg Company followed the tracks of others on the Southern Trail toward the Pima villages.

Cox entertains the reader with his August 21 attempt to kill one of the wild bulls at the San Bernardino Rancho in Sonora, Mexico: "the old fellow seemed bullet proof. At each report of the Rifle he would but shake himself and charge again—the engagement was long and sanguinary . . .

but finally he fell—and with a last long lingering heave gave up the Ghost—" Cox does not neglect to talk about people he met along the way and writes about encounters with James Collier *(33)*, John W. Audubon *(18)*, and Cave Couts *(106)*. Lew B. Harris *(53)* was also a member of this group of emigrants. As a matter of fact, Harris, who later became county clerk of Sacramento, hired Cox to be his deputy.

Cox soon tired of California and returned to Texas, where he purchased a ranch, a store, and a lumber yard. In 1886 he was elected judge for Live Oak County. The Cox diaries make good reading in addition to presenting a thorough account of the trip. [TT-ST-GT]

37. CREIGHTON, MARY LEE (PATRICK), ca. 1842–?

"Reminiscences, San Francisco, September 8, 1915." Typescript memoirs in the Bancroft Library.

Mary Lee Creighton, daughter of J. W. Patrick, was seven years old in 1849 when her parents joined the Clarksville (Arkansas) wagon train for the trip to California. As a result, her memoirs are sketchy except for her vivid recollection of what eventually became a well-publicized event along the trail: the Hickey-Davis stabbing and execution, which is described in the section, "Forty-niners on the Gila Trail." She remained in California and attended Mrs. Hammond's Seminary with Mary Donner, a survivor of the unforgettable winter in the Sierra Nevada. She later married Samuel Gray Creighton. Her photograph, taken in 1861, appeared in the *Little Rock Arkansas Gazette* re-publication of the Alfred D. King diary on March 9, 1941 *(65)*. [FS-ST-GT]

38. CRUMPTON, HEZEKIAH JOHN, 1823–?

The Adventures of Two Alabama Boys. Montgomery, Ala.: The Paragon Press, 1912.

Part 1 of the volume contains the reminiscences of Dr. Hezekiah J. Crumpton's trip to California via the Fort Smith–Santa Fe and Southern trails. He rode out of Fort Smith on April 12, 1849, following Captain Randolph Marcy and his troops. He was flat broke on his arrival in Los Angeles, but was lucky enough to go to work for the California ranchero Abel Stearns until he earned enough to pay for a mining outfit. Crumpton started prospecting in the spring of 1850 and sojourned in Nevada City, California, where he earned his living at Caldwell's store until 1853, when he returned to New Orleans to complete his medical education.

According to his biography (HNL 1881:224–225), he moved back to

California with his degree and settled in Lake County. He was elected to the California state legislature in 1880. Parts 2 and 3 contain the memoirs of his brother, W. B. Crumpton, which tell the story of his trip to California via Panama in 1849 and a return trip to California after a forty-year absence. [FS-ST-GT]

39.   DAWSON, NICHOLAS "CHEYENNE," 1819–1903

Narrative. San Francisco: Grabhorn Press, 1933.

This finely printed book contains memoirs of a colorful character whose life spanned eighty-three years. Dawson's first trip to California was with the Bidwell party in 1841. He returned home to Sherman, Texas, soon caught "gold fever," and headed for California one more time, leaving on March 1, 1849. He took the same difficult route John Audubon *(18)* would take in April—the treacherous mule trail across the Sierra Madre Occidental to Altar, Sonora—but without the difficulty since he was an experienced traveler, well prepared, and took the whole thing in stride. He arrived in the Mariposa diggings around November 1, 1849.

Job Dye *(44)* hired him to work in his Santa Cruz, California, store for a time, but Dawson was not through wandering. He wrote *California in '41 Texas in '51* (New York: The Pemberton Press, 1969), which repeated some of his adventures from 1849 but dealt mostly with his later life. [MX-GT]

40.   DEADERICK, DAVID A.

"Diary." Typescript in the James D. Hoskins Library, the University of Tennessee, Knoxville, Libraries. Some Deaderick letters are contained in the James G. Ramsey Papers at the University of Tennessee.

David Deaderick was a member of the East Tennessee Mining Company, headed by Alexander Outlaw Anderson, and was a good friend of Wilberforce Ramsey *(78)*, whose letters are cited here. He left a four-page typescript that briefly outlined the route to California along the Southern Trail. Deaderick returned to Knoxville in March 1851 and settled down to a job in the Miners and Manufacturers Bank. [SF-ST-GT]

41.   DEMAREST, DAVID DURIE, 1824–1912

"Diary, March 8, 1849–May 1850, of a Trip in a Bark Norumbega to Galveston, Texas, then Overland to California." Typescript in the Bancroft Library.

Demarest and fellow members of the P. F. Smith Company sailed from New York on March 8, 1849, for Galveston, Texas. This traveler manages to provide the essential facts in each of his brief entries, and the reader can easily follow his trip. His is one of the useful accounts of travel across Texas on the Upper Emigrant Road to Coons' Ranch by way of San Antonio, Austin, and Fredericksburg. The diary is of particular interest because he joined a company headed by Texas Ranger John Coffee Hays *(55)*, near San Diego Mound on the Rio Grande. The Frémont Association of New York also attached themselves to this group.

The men followed Philip St. George Cooke's *(104)* route on the Southern Trail as far as Soldier's Farewell (formerly Ben Moore Mountain), where they bumped into Mexican General José María Elías. On October 15, 1849, Demarest wrote that "in a long conversation that Hays had with the General, he asked him if he supposed that we could go on a due-west course from here to Tucson, instead of going on the road that runs far to the south. The General said he thought we could and he left two guides for that purpose." This shortened the trip considerably. The new cutoff would ultimately become known as the Apache Pass Trail.

Demarest mined until about 1860, when he purchased the Altaville Foundry and Machine Shops in Angels Camp, California (MBHCM 1892:211). He kept numerous diaries over time, but those written prior to 1860 were lost in the 1923 Berkeley fire, according to his son in a note on the typescript diary. [TT-AP-GT]

42.   DURIVAGE, JOHN E., ?–1869

"Through Mexico to California. Letters and Journals of John E. Durivage," edited by Ralph P. Bieber. *Southern Trails To California in 1849*. Vol. 5, Southwest Historical Series. Glendale, Calif.: The Arthur H. Clark Company, 1937. Pp. 159–255.

Employed by the *New Orleans Daily Picayune* to report on the overland experience, John Durivage embarked for Rio Grande City, Texas, on March 4, 1849. He proceeded westward through Mexico by way of Monterrey, Saltillo, Chihuahua, and Janos before joining the Southern Trail at Guadalupe Pass. Durivage's tales of adventure not only make exciting reading but provide excellent descriptive material that helps relocate the original trail.

Here is another pioneer, described as a man with an ardent and generous disposition, who left his mark in California. He soon became acting secretary of the 1st California Guard (California Artillery 1850) and was among the founders of the San Francisco paper *Alta California*. He wrote his farewell to San Francisco in that paper on October 15, 1851, then spent the next twenty years writing for the press in Boston, New Orleans, New York, and California. At the same time, he was a noted and popular comedian (Brown 1969:411; *Alta California* 9/22/1856). [TM-ST-GT]

43.   DUVAL, ISAAC, 1824–1902

Texas Argonauts: Isaac H. Duval and the California Gold Rush, edited by Richard H. Dillon, illustrated by Charles Shaw. San Francisco: The Book Club of California, 1987. A shorter version was published as "Overland to California," edited by Gary C. Stein. *American History Illustrated* 12 (1977):26–36. The original manuscript is in possession of the Duval family.

Duval wrote his memoirs in the 1890s, and Richard Dillon has expertly edited the most recent edition. Duval was a no-nonsense leader of men but in spite of discipline (or perhaps because of it) faced numerous incidents that challenged the spirit. This company left Panola County, Texas, and headed for El Paso del Norte, by way of Dallas, Waco, Odessa, the Guadalupe Mountains (Texas), and Hueco Tanks. They turned south at El Paso, passing the Mexican towns of Corralitos and Janos before joining the Southern Trail at Guadalupe Pass. Excitement was running high in these tiny frontier towns, where Duval and his men had encounters with both the Apache Indians and Mexican troops, the latter trying to subdue the former.

He appeared to be an inveterate sightseer as well and is the only traveler of record who took time out to visit and describe the prehistoric Hohokam site Casa Grande, near the Pima villages in Arizona. They arrived safely at Isaac Williams's Rancho Santa Ana del Chino on August 26, 1849, and before leaving for the mines, left their names in his "Register Book" *(102)*. Dillon has provided a very good map of the route.

Duval subsequently served in the U.S. Army, retiring in 1866 with the rank of general. After the close of the Civil War, he was elected Republican member of both houses of the West Virginia legislature, and from 1869 to 1871 served as congressman in the U.S. House of Representatives. He ultimately settled in Arkadelphia, Arkansas, with his wife and ten children. [TM-ST-GT]

First page from the Register of the Rancho Santa Ana del Chino,
showing William Goulding's August 12 entry. The second entry was
made on August 17 by Jack W. Smith, with the Isaac Duval company.
Courtesy, the Huntington Library.

44.   DYE, JOB FRANCIS, 1807–1883

Recollections of a Pioneer 1830-1852: Rocky Mountains, New Mexico, California. Los Angeles: Glen Dawson, 1951. *Santa Cruz (Calif.) Sentinel,* May 1, 8, 15, 22, and June 5, 12, 19, 1869; part of the Job Francis Dye Pioneer Scrapbook (1869–1876) in the Bancroft Library.

Dye was an experienced frontiersman who arrived in California with the Ewing Young expedition in 1832. During the gold rush excitement, he went into business with Thomas O. Larkin (consul for the United States in Monterey, California), and anticipating demands by miners, sailed often to Mazatlán, where he purchased goods for sale in San Francisco. He tells us that he bought 300 mules in 1849, which he expected to sell to miners. He does not detail his return trip, but his narrative is included because he herded the animals through Sonora toward the Yuma Crossing on the Colorado. That journey would have required travel over that infamous highway, El Camino del Diablo, during June and July, when temperatures topped 120 degrees and travelers needed a couple of gallons of water a day just to survive.

Dye wrote that he hired twenty-five New Yorkers (probably gold-seekers down on their luck in Mexico) to guard the train as they proceeded toward Yuma. He also claimed to be the first to cross and describe New River (near Seely in the California desert), which had not run in over fifty years. That stream was dry when Cooke's and Kearny's troops passed in 1846, "but to our agreeable surprise," Dye said, "when in the middle of he desert at midnight we came to a New River, which providentially had been . . . formed by back water from the Colorado, and . . . I was the first white man that crossed it and gave to the world a description of its extent" (*Santa Cruz Sentinel,* 6/5/1869). Goldseekers coming off the Southern and Gila trails would also have much to say about that life-saving river in the desert. Dye ultimately retired to his farm near Santa Cruz, California. [DH]

45.   ECCLESTON, ROBERT, 1830–1911

Overland to California on the Southwestern Trail of 1849, edited by George P. Hammond and Edward P. Howes. Los Angeles: University of California Press, 1950. The Eccleston diaries are in the Bancroft Library.

Eccleston joined the Frémont Association in New York and traveled by both land and sea to Port Lavaca, Texas. Before leaving New York, the association arranged to travel with John Coffee Hays *(55)*, who had been assigned to survey a new road to Coons' Ranch and El Paso del Norte by way of San Antonio and the Las Moras River. It was later known as the Lower or Military Road. Continuing overland, the company arrived at Coons' Ranch on September 8, 1849, and prepared to move to California on the Southern Trail. Eccleston carefully penned the details of this trip, thus leaving a fine record of the opening of the road. His diary contains another first since Hays and the company charted a new cutoff for Tucson, the Apache Pass Trail. Eccleston made his last entry on December 22, 1849, while resting at New River, California.

Though the map accompanying the text traces the route of the Frémont Association by way of Apache Pass correctly, it incorrectly traces a segment of the Southern Trail paralleling the New Mexico border to the international boundary from north to south. This is a topographic impossibility since the argonauts would have had to walk across the tops of the Guadalupe range in Arizona, instead of snaking over Guadalupe Pass.

The young traveler also kept a number of diaries describing his sojourn in the mines. These were published under the title *The Mariposa Indian War of 1850–1851,* edited by C. Gregory Crampton (University of Utah Press, 1975). According to editor George P. Hammond, Robert Eccleston married Emily Josephine Young in 1857, and they settled in Butte County for a time. We do not know how Eccleston earned his living, but records show that his children were born in Forbestown, California; New York City; Bergen Heights, New Jersey; and Tucson and Tombstone, Arizona. [TT-AP-GT]

46.   EVANS, GEORGE W. B., 1819–1850

Mexican Gold Trail, the Journal of a Forty Niner, edited by Glenn S. Dumke. San Marino, Calif.: The Huntington Library, 1945. The Evans manuscript is in the Huntington Library.

Evans began his California journey on February 20, 1849, and traveled with the Defiance (Ohio) Gold Hunters' Expedition. One of his traveling companions, Dr. Lafayette Bunnell, would later report on the 1851 discovery of the Yosemite Valley. This group of goldseekers sailed to Port Lavaca, Texas, then moved overland to Eagle Pass on the Rio Grande. They hired a guide here to lead them west over the barren uplands of the Serranías del Burro, one of the few groups on record to chance that route. The men rejoined the established road at Chihuahua and reached the Guadalupe Pass trailhead in early August. In addition to being an accurate daily record of events, the Evans diary is well written and full of description, history, and adventure.

Evans added his name to the "Register" at the Rancho Santa Ana del Chino on September 16, 1849 *(102)*, before leaving for the Agua Fria diggings. He arrived in that southern mining camp on October 29, 1849. He died during a cholera epidemic that swept Sacramento in December 1850.

The editor has used John Bartlett's sketch from *Personal Narrative (97)* that illustrates Guadalupe Pass in New Mexico, but has incorrectly used Lewis B. Harris's account of his June 18 trip over Guadalupe Pass in Texas (*53* 1926:218) to describe the New Mexico land form. There are also some errors in the accompanying map, including the mislocation of Guadalupe Pass, New Mexico, and the San Bernardino Rancho and Santa Cruz in Sonora. [MX-ST-GT]

47.   FAIRCHILD, JOHN A., 1829–?

"John A. Fairchild Biographical Sketch." Original and microfilm copy in the Bancroft Library.

Fairchild's brief reminiscences are far from satisfactory. He leaves us with enough information, however, to confirm that he left Texas on April 17, 1849, with the Cherokee Company commanded by a Captain Carter. The company followed the Southern Trail to San Diego. A traveling companion was the hot-tempered Texas Ranger David S. Terry, who later served as chief justice of the California Supreme Court but was best remembered for fatally wounding Senator David C. Broderick in 1859 in the last of the great duels fought in California. Fairchild eventually settled in Yreka, California. [TM-ST-GT]

48.   FORSYTH, JOHN ROBERT, 1802–1860

"Diary." Manuscript (1849) in the Peoria, Illinois, Public Library. There is a typescript in the Bancroft Library.

Forsyth left Peoria on April 5, 1849. Led by frontiersman James Kirker, the Peoria Company embarked on the Santa Fe Trail at Fort Leavenworth, Kansas. After a brief stop in Santa Fe, the men continued to California on the Southern Trail, arriving on December 3, 1849.

This is a beautifully written, detailed daily account amounting to some 65,000 words. Forsyth was curious about everything and embraced life with gusto. As if the walk across country was not enough, he took time to climb mountains. He visited Indian families and talked with them. He described plants, animals, and towns and villages. Nothing escaped his notice. On May 25, near a Kaw village [Kansa Tribe] he wrote, "It was certainly picturesque to see the Braves sweeping round on their Horses in their Red Blankets one eye painted Red another Black or Blue the nose a bright vermilion. Long feathers in their pen. On scalp lock, Bow and Arrows. Bridle covered with small Bells. Horses Tail plaited full of Ribons & Feathers, a Gun across in saddle Bow. Belts of wampum. . ." He left an equally graphic description of the Papago (Tohono O'odham) scalp dance that he witnessed on October 4 when he arrived at San Xavier del Bac. William Hunter *(62)* also left his version of the event.

Forsyth's diary ends mid-page in San Diego, but according to a short sketch by his granddaughter, he arrived in San Francisco in January of 1850. She wrote little about his later activities except that he died suddenly from a burst appendix while on a hunting trip after his return to Peoria. [SF-ST-GT]

49.   FOUTS, D. LAMBERT

"Diary, 1849 and records, 1861–1863." Manuscript in Holt-Atherton Department of Special Collections, University of the Pacific Libraries, Stockton, California, attributed to D. Lambert Fouts. It is accompanied by an inaccurate type-script provided by the donor. Accurate typescript (carbon of the holograph diary) is in the Bancroft Library, attributed to Caspar Stinemets Ricks *(80)*. The donor of the holograph diary at University of the Pacific believes that D. Lambert Fouts is the author. Beginning pages are missing but several names are written in front by someone other than the diarist. They are: "D. Lambert Fouts," "Ricks," and "Bill Etter." A number of pages have been used for other data.

Now, here is the mystery: The Bancroft Library has long had an accurate carbon typescript of the same diary. The contents compare favorably with the original at University of the Pacific. Front pages, if any, are missing, but penciled on top is "Ricks - diary of a trip thru North Mexico." Provenance is unknown. Back in 1929, when Owen Coy quoted this diary extensively in *The Great Trek (107)*, he attributed authorship to Caspar Stinemets Ricks, founder of the city of Eureka. I postulate that

Coy made the copy that found its way to the Bancroft. However, Ricks could not have written the diary because he landed in California by way of Panama on August 18, 1849 (Irvine 1915:232), while the writer of this little volume was in the village of Santa Cruz, Sonora, on August 9, 1849.

We learn from Leigh Irvine (1915:236) that Caspar Ricks had a brother-in-law by the name of Daniel L. Fouts (D. Lambert?), who was born in 1823, came to California in 1853, and settled in San Francisco. He was employed as a clerk in the office of the Indian agent and died in 1893. It is possible that Fouts had also made a trip in 1849, which was not recorded in the county history. On the other hand, we may never know who authored this little book and how it came to be in the Ricks family.

This overland saga opened near Santa Fe, New Mexico. The author wrote that he teamed up with Robert Brownlee *(27)* and other members of the Little Rock Company for the remainder of the trip to California. We learn that the diarist had been suffering with chills and diarrhea for two weeks when he recorded his final entry on August 10, 1849, while in the village of Santa Cruz, Sonora: "we traveled rapidly we passed a deserted ranch situated on a creek at which was a noble peach orchard, the first peaches I had seen since time I had left home or even then - we traveled about 16 miles and camped in a most beautiful valley good grass the cottonwoods in a string and remarkably tall . . . " There are four unreadable lines on the following page. Since he had been faithfully recording his daily adventures, I question his fate when his reminiscences end mid-page and mid-sentence.

The manuscript is excellent for retracing the trip between Albuquerque and Santa Cruz and includes detailed sketches of his traveling companions. [FS-ST-GT]

50.   GOODING, LARRY, 1831–?

"Across the Plains in 1849," *Frontier Times* 1 (August 1924):1–6. Taken from the *Dallas News,* May 14, 1911.

Grant Foreman (*116*:147) wrote that Lawrence S. Gooding, a merchant from the village of Doaksville, which was near Fort Towson where Captain Randolph B. Marcy was stationed, accompanied the troops to Santa Fe and back to Fort Smith. If the *Frontier Times* story is true, Gooding persuaded Marcy to take his eighteen-year-old son, Larry, on the trip. This was high adventure for the young man, and although he said little about the trip to Santa Fe, he vividly detailed the Indian ambush and murder of one of Marcy's men, Lieutenant Montgomery Pike Harrison, and the reconstruction of the crime by the Indian guide, Black Beaver. Gooding returned to Fort Smith with the troops on a more southerly route between Doña Ana and Fort Washita. This is among the few accounts that have come to light that recount a trip on Marcy's return route. [FS-]

51.   GOULDING, WILLIAM R., 1807–?

"Journal, March 10–September 18, 1849." Manuscript in the Yale Collection of Western Americana, Beinecke Rare Book and Manuscript Library.

Here is a colorful and lengthy diary, filled with good detail, plenty of ethnographic material, and numerous interesting anecdotes. Goulding divided the 377 handwritten pages into twenty-one chapters, which were organized from an earlier diary for publication at a later date. Included are sketches of a Comanche family and a broadside containing the constitution of the Knickerbocker Exploring Company of New York, with the names and addresses of its 110 members.

The company kept fairly close to Captain Randolph Marcy and his roadbuilding troops on the Fort Smith–Santa Fe Trail but split up on reaching Santa Fe; half the members opted for a pack trip over the Gila Trail. Goulding was among those who kept to the Southern Trail, arriving at the Rancho Santa Ana del Chino on August 12, 1849.

He achieved distinction by making the first entry in Isaac Williams's "Rancho Santa Ana del Chino Register Book" *(102)*, where he described his trip in detail. Moreover, it appears that he set up columns in his own handwriting so others could add their names as they came along. As a matter of fact, because Goulding spent a number of days with Isaac Williams and became his good friend, I postulate that it was Goulding's idea to have the oncoming overlanders sign the "Register."

Of particular interest is Goulding's description of Isaac Williams and his life on the rancho. He describes how Williams put up General Kearny's Army of the West back in 1846 and how Colonel Frémont had offered to purchase his land. Goulding has some interesting things to say in a September 16 letter to Williams about his later meeting with Frémont on behalf of Williams. Though most of what Goulding wrote is substantiated, a researcher is advised to be vigilant. On May 27, 1849, Goulding copied Lieutenant William Emory's 1846 description of

Pecos Pueblo verbatim, which ended with the sentence: "The cornices and drops of the architrave in the modern church are elaborately carved with a knife..." (*114*:30).

Some time later, Goulding returned east and was appointed to the U.S. Medical Museum in Washington. [FS-ST-GT]

52.   HARRIS, BENJAMIN BUTLER, 1824–1897

The Gila Trail. The Texas Argonauts and the California Gold Rush, edited by Richard H. Dillon. Norman: University of Oklahoma Press, 1960. Second printing, 1984. Original manuscript is in the Huntington Library.

The title misleads since Harris did not join the Gila Trail until he arrived at the Pima villages. Because he was writing some forty years after the fact, he could recall his adventure with a different perspective and thus inject a goodly amount of humor. As a result, he gives us a delightful read. Harris writes that he joined Isaac Duval *(43)* and his company leaving Panola County, Texas, on March 25, 1849. After stopping at El Paso del Norte, the men turned south into Mexico, and followed the Corralitos-Janos road toward the trailhead near Guadalupe Pass. He signed in at the Rancho Santa Ana del Chino on August 26, 1849. Harris and his fellow goldseekers rode to the mines via the San Fernando Valley in California and dismounted at Bear Creek on September 29, 1849.

The accompanying map is incorrect in a number of places. Guadalupe Pass has been placed in Sonora between Agua Prieta and Janos, and the trail out of Yuma is shown as going over the Algodones Dunes in California rather than by way of Paredones in Baja, California.

Harris practiced law in Mariposa for a time but left to enlist in the Confederate army. After the war, he returned to California and settled in San Bernardino. Charles Perry, Harris's great-grandson, drove to Yuma in 1988 to retrace his grandfather's journey from the Colorado Crossing to Mariposa. Afterwards he wrote "Back to the Gold Rush: In Which the Author Retraces the Steps of His Great-Grandfather in 1849, When Things Looked Mighty Different in California," *Los Angeles Times Magazine*, July 3, 1988. [TM-ST-GT]

53.   HARRIS, LEWIS BIRDSALL, 1816–1893

"Overland by Boat to California," edited by Aurora Hunt. *The Historical Society of Southern California Quarterly* 31

(1949):212–218. "Letters to Brother," *Southwestern Historical Quarterly* 29 (1926):215–223. "Up From San Antonio," edited by Wilmer B. Shields. *San Diego Historical Society Quarterly* 9 (January 1963):1–6.

Lewis B. Harris built his wagon bed in the shape of a boat and painted it green. We learn that he was generous with his "boat," having assisted several companies across the Pecos, the Rio Grande, and the Colorado. Lieutenant Cave Couts offered Harris $75 for his wagon at the Yuma Crossing, but it was still in good shape, and Harris moved on to the mines with his "green boat" intact.

This company rolled along the Upper Road from San Antonio, Texas. Soon after arriving at Coons' Ranch, it turned north and followed the Rio Grande to the Southern Trail junction near Garfield, New Mexico. On November 7, 1849, Harris made the following entry in the "Rancho Santa Ana del Chino Register Book" *(102)*: "arrived here from Harris County Texas, Lewis B. Harris & lady." The above articles are based on Harris's letters to his brother, which are located in the California State Library.

Harris spent the rest of his life serving California. He was sheriff, county clerk, and mayor of Sacramento; deputy secretary of state of California; and then retired to San Diego, where he sold insurance. [TT-ST-GT]

54. HAYES, BENJAMIN IGNATIUS, 1815–1877

Pioneer Notes from the Diaries of Judge Benjamin Hayes, edited by Marjorie Tisdale Wolcott. Los Angeles: Marjorie Tisdale Wolcott, 1929. Hayes's notebooks are in the Bancroft Library.

Most forty-niners packed too many luxuries—gold washing machines and the like—which were discarded long before the journey was over. Benjamin Hayes, however, had to be very careful with supplies since a good friend lent him $200 for his outfit and two mules and tossed in another $50 for expenses. Thus Hayes's pack included only absolute necessities, among them twenty-seven yards of red flannel and calico for the Indians.

He started out on the Santa Fe Trail from Independence, Missouri, on September 10, 1849. His party bypassed Santa Fe and angled south to Socorro on the Rio Grande by way of Galisteo, Quarai, and Abo. They continued along the Southern Trail, arriving in Los Angeles on February 26, 1850. Hayes's meticulous notes help us relive some dramatic moments in the western desert since he recorded many meetings with a variety of individuals he met along the way.

Judge Hayes remained in California, where he became a prominent and respected jurist and civic leader. During this time, he stored his reminiscences in hundreds of scrapbooks, which are in the Bancroft Library.[SF-ST-GT]

55.   HAYS, JOHN COFFEE, 1817–1883

"Life and Adventures of John C. Hays, the Texas Ranger." Dictation by Hays and close friend, John Caperton, for Hubert Howe Bancroft. Manuscript (1879) in the Bancroft Library.

The account covers Hays's experience as a soldier and Texas Ranger during the Mexican War. It provides sketchy information on the overland experience but does verify key portions of the route. Hays was on his way west to assume his new appointment as Indian sub-agent on the Gila River. Instead, he continued on to California, became sheriff of San Francisco, and founded the city of Oakland. Details of the trip are contained in Robert Eccleston's diary *(45)* and the John Nugent *(71)* and David Demarest *(41)* accounts. [TT-AP-GT]

56.   HESLEP, AUGUSTUS M., 1806–1885

"The Santa Fe Trail. Journals and Letters of Augustus M. Heslep," edited by Ralph P. Bieber. *Southern Trails to California in 1849.* Vol. 5, Southwest Historical Series. Glendale, Calif.: The Arthur H. Clark Company, 1937. Pp. 353–386.

Dr. Heslep left his medical practice in St. Louis to chance a trip to California. He started out from Independence, Missouri, on May 15, 1849, with the Morgan County and California Rangers of Illinois, and traveled over the Santa Fe and Southern trails. Heslep's series of letters were first printed in issues of the *Daily Missouri Republican*, and since he was writing for publication, he apparently worked hard to write colorful vignettes: "A storm on the prairies," he said, "presents a sublime and fearful sight . . . In a few moments a fearful strife of the elements was at work. The lightning's flash . . . was grand but awful; the roar of heaven's artillery was deafening; and amidst the din and war of the elements, the very floodgates of heaven seemd to be opened upon us in a drenching and soaking rain" (p. 363). The doctor passed Los Angeles on December 13, 1849, and posted his last letter in San Jose on January 24, 1850.

Heslep married Josephine Morrow of San Francisco in 1856 (*Alta California*, 9/6/1856) and remained in that city until his death in 1885 (CSL). [SF-ST-GT]

57. HOBBS, JAMES

Wild Life in the Far West; Personal Adventures of a Border Man. Hartford, Conn.: Wiley, Waterman & Eaton, 1874.

This one-of-a-kind character claims to have had numerous adventures with "Kit Carson and others; captivity and life among the Comanches; Services under Doniphan in the War with Mexico, and in the Mexican War against the French; Desperate Combats with Apaches, Grizzly Bears, etc., etc."

Hobbs was in Zacatecas, Mexico, when California gold fever broke out, and he "became infected with the disease!" He further noted that he stitched his $8,000 into a Mexican packsaddle and headed for the Colorado Crossing at Yuma over El Camino del Diablo. Then he went on to Los Angeles and the mines. This is not a book that will give any help on locating the route followed, but does contribute some 400 delightful pages promoting the myth of the West. [DH]

58. HUBBARD, CAL, 1815–1859

"The Devil's Highway," by Tom Bailey. *True West* 7 (November–December 1959):7–8, 42–45.

Cal Hubbard probably did open a successful rooming house in Placerville and go into the merchandising business in Sacramento after arrival in California. It is also possible that he was involved with the building of the Southern Pacific by providing backing to Theodore Judah. The rest of the overland story, however, comes off as bad fiction. We learn that Hubbard and eighty-five travelers from Memphis were in such fear of the Apaches that they decided to take El Camino del Diablo in southern Arizona. The 130-mile stretch to Yuma crossed a desolate area with few water sources; it would have been pure foolishness to attempt the trip in summer, which this group said they did. We are told that a number of travelers perished from thirst. We are further asked to believe that among the group were several villainous types who plotted to lose the party in the desert waste and return to gather the spoils after they all died from thirst! This is one of three accounts by forty-niners who may have negotiated that lonely, parched trail. It was, of course, the favored route of thousands of Sonorans who went to the mines. [DH]

59.   HUDGINS, JOHN, 1826–1910

"California in 1849," edited by Adrienne Christopher. *Westport Historical Quarterly* 6(1970):3–16. The journal is repeated without notes in *One Hundred Years in Livingston County*. Chillicothe, Mo.: n.p., 1976, pp. 41–47.

Hudgins recalled that he left Livingston County, Missouri, on May 6, 1849. He and his fellow travelers teamed up with a company from Illinois near Council Grove, then trod along the Santa Fe Trail to Las Vegas, New Mexico, where they turned west on the Southern Trail. This traveler arrived at New River, California, on Christmas Day, then continued to the mines on foot by way of the San Fernando Valley. Though his story is short, he covers a few pages describing the boat he constructed out of abandoned wagon beds, then tells how he loaded 5,500 pounds of freight before sailing his boat down the Gila River to its junction with the Colorado.

In 1850 Hudgins was hired by a group of Los Angeles businessmen to work on a trail that bridged the principal rivers in Tulare County (MHTC 1974:19). But by 1852, Hudgins had had enough of California and went back to Missouri, where he hired on as a mail carrier until he retired to his farm near Mooresville. [SF-ST]

60.   HUFF, WILLIAM P., ?–1886

"From the Santa Cruz to the Gila in 1850: An Excerpt From the Overland Journal of William P. Huff," edited by John Hosmer and the students from Tucson's University High School and Green Fields Country Day School. *Journal of Arizona History* 32 (Spring 1991):41–110. According to editor Hosmer, the manuscript, "Journal of William P. Huff on an Overland Trip from Richmond, Fort Bend County, Texas, to Mariposa in Southern California in the Years 1849 and 1850," belongs to David Ewing Stewart of Van Vleck, Texas. An incomplete typescript is in Patricia Etter's files.

The published portion of the journal covers the journey of Huff and the Socorro (Texas) Company through Arizona. The work contains one of the only accounts in English of Tucson's last Mexican *commandante* and presents an interesting look at Texas's first provisional governor, Henry W. Smith, who traveled with the group.

This is probably one of the most detailed journals in existence, containing some 300,000 words. There is good evidence to suggest that Huff wrote this version (including embellishments) about 1873 from earlier notes. The reader is warned to watch for inconsistencies. For example, it appears that this diarist consulted John Bartlett's narrative *(97)* and incorporated some descriptive elements into his own work. On the other hand, the manuscript contains some delightful, though unsubstantiated, vignettes including an incredible description of an evening of monte with the locals in Socorro, Texas.

Huff left Fredericksburg in June of 1849 and wintered in Socorro, Texas, before starting out again for California in February 1850. He crossed the Rio Grande and headed for Samalayuca on the Corralitos-Janos road, then connected with the southern trailhead at Guadalupe Pass. One of Huff's traveling companions, C. H. Veeder, signed the "Register Book" at the Rancho Santa Ana del Chino on May 23, 1850, after recording some serious problems with the Yuma Indians at the Colorado *(102)*.

Early on Huff showed a real interest in anthropology and archaeology, and when he unearthed the first recognized Pleistocene vertebrates in Texas, his discovery caused an international stir. His collection ultimately found its way to the British Museum, where it remains. Huff returned to Fredericksburg with little to show for his prospecting efforts. He married and went into the retail business like his father before him.

Hosmer and his students received the James F. Elliott II Award for the article at the Arizona History Convention in Prescott, 1992. [TM-ST-GT]

61.   HUNTER, ROBERT, 1813-1856

A Texan in the Gold Rush: The Letters of Robert Hunter 1849–1851, edited by Robert W. Stephens. Bryan, Tex.: Barnum and White Publications, Inc., 1972.

The slim volume reproduces letters that Robert Hunter wrote to his wife, Cyrene Sutton Hunter, during his trip to the gold country. We learn that he started out from Fayette County, Texas, and was in Fredericksburg by April 23. His letters give very little information about the cross-country experience except that he trod the Southern Trail, had a short skirmish with Apache Indians near the Gila River, and added his name to the "Register Book" at the Rancho Santa Ana del Chino on September 2, 1849 *(102)*. Hunter went on to mines in northern California and in 1851 joined John J. Kuykendall's Company A, Mariposa Battalion, to hunt Indians who were committing depredations in Mariposa County.

The editor writes that Hunter took an overland route on his return to Leon County Texas in 1852. He died of pneumonia four years later. [TT-ST-GT]

62.   HUNTER, WILLIAM W.

Missouri 49er. The Journal of William W. Hunter on the Southern Gold Trail, edited by David P. Robrock. Albuquerque: University of New Mexico Press, 1992. Original diary and transcript are in the Special Collections Library, University of Arizona.

This is an outstanding, detailed journal that carefully traces the trip from Montgomery County, Missouri, along the Santa Fe and Southern trails. Hunter describes every camp site, counts the number of miles traveled each day, and adds some fine comments on the trail. On September 15, 1849, for example, he was in Guadalupe Canyon, where he found "some of the most wild and rugged scenery imaginable. At every turn of the Creek some new feature was presented tending to add grandeur or sublimity to the vista, while the beautiful green canopy above shielded us from the rays of the sun . . ." Additionally, he adds rare ethnographic observations including a description of the Papago (Tohono O'odham) scalp dance at Mission San Xavier del Bac, which he witnessed on October 4.

Robrock was unable to uncover any information about Hunter's past or his ultimate fate. However, Hunter's description of landforms was so accurate, it allowed members of Southwest Oregon-California Trails Association to identify the exact spot that emigrants left the Rio Grande, a few miles north of Garfield, New Mexico, in April 1996. Since the trail was in an unnamed wash, it was called Hunter's Draw in honor of the argonaut (Tompkins 1996). [SF-ST-GT]

63.   IRBY, BENJAMIN F., ca. 1826–?

"Pathfinders of '49," by Mrs. Alfred Irby. *The Overland Monthly* 69 (January–June 1917):171 174.

There appears to be no doubt that Irby was a real character and did travel to California from Texas along the Southern Trail in 1849. It is not known if the author was writing from notes, but we can say that there are a number of problems with the story. For example: Yuma Indians were to be found at the Colorado River, not the Pecos; he would have arrived at an "old mission" (San Xavier del Bac or Tumacacori) before arrival at the Pima villages; the Pima Indians did not raise barley, and finally, no emigrants ever traveled down a long stretch in the Grand Canyon! [TT-ST-GT]

64.   JORDAN, DAVID, 1805–1857

"Dr. David Jordan. Diary, 1849." Paper copy from microfilm in the California State Library, Sacramento. "Notes by the Way." Paper copies from microfilm (1849) in the Bancroft Library.

There is no doubt that the above documents are exact duplicates. Both copies contain a manuscript note by granddaughter Mary A. Jordan Hackenberger with an account of Jordan's subsequent years. The Bancroft copy contains a photo of the diarist.

Dr. David Jordan journeyed from Dayton, Ohio, to Fort Smith, Arkansas, then set out on the trail for California on March 27, 1849, arriving at the Mariposa diggings on September 8, 1849. He writes a good story and is candid about what life on the trail is really like. We cannot help but smile when we learn that on April 13, he hung his "new fustian pantaloons near the fire to dry" and a puff of wind carried them off into his campfire. On Monday, April 16, he wrote that his horse mired and fell, and as it struggled to stand up threw Jordan over its head into the mud.

Jordan is the only overlander who recorded arrival at some hot springs on the road between the Mimbres River and Cow Springs in New Mexico. "This is quite a curiosity," he wrote on June 23, "There are several springs bursting out at the base of a large mound, the water of which is quite warm, on the top of the mound is a pool about 25 or 30 feet in diameter & 10 or 12 feet deep, the water so hot that you can not bear your hand in it more than a few seconds..." This place, which was settled the following year, became known as Faywood Springs. It is north of Deming, on New Mexico 61.

According to Hackenberger, Jordan amassed a fortune mining but was held up by Mexican bandits and robbed. Not one to give up easily, he went back to the mines and dug another fortune. This time, he boarded a ship for home, but it sunk along with his money. Jordan survived, but his third effort to reap golden treasure failed. So he went home, where he died before he could bring his family back to California. [FS-ST-GT]

65.   KING, ALFRED D., 1824–1897

"Alfred D. King Journal, 1849" (second half, July 6–December 22, 1849). Manuscript in the Special Collections Library, University of Arkansas, Fayetteville. A second version, "Trip to the Gold Fields," edited by S. H. Logan, *Little Rock Arkansas Gazette*, Sunday magazine section, in twenty-four weekly installments starting January 19, 1941. A microfilm copy of this version is in the Bancroft Library.

Alfred D. King was a member of the Clarksville (Arkansas) and California Mining Association that left Fort Smith, Arkansas, on April 11, 1849, and traveled in tandem with Captain Randolph Marcy and his troops. The holograph document at the University of Arkansas was written by King and contains good detail. It begins July 6 on the banks of the Rio Grande near Socorro, New Mexico. King wrote that the first part of his diary was in another volume, which has not been located.

S. H. Logan of Clarksville, Arkansas, editor of the work published in the *Arkansas Gazette*, claimed that he copied the material from the original first half of the King journal (April–July), which he claimed was in his possession (as mentioned above, it has not been located). Researchers are advised to approach with caution. Logan copied Captain Marcy's notes from *Marcy and the Goldseekers (116)*. In addition, a chapter has been taken from Josiah Gregg's *Commerce of the Prairies (117)*. Moreover, the first half contains numerous dramatic vignettes about Indian tribes and life along the trail which cannot be verified. The second half of the published work is Logan's rewritten version of King's holograph manuscript in which he made numerous editorial changes. The published version does include photographs of members of the train.

King also drew a detailed map of the journey between the Colorado River to San Diego and Los Angeles. George Ellis (1996) believes that King copied it from one of the the hundreds of waybill maps that Cave Couts drew for emigrants arriving at the Colorado Crossing, and it may be the only copy that has survived. This is possible since both King and Couts were at the Colorado on October 1 and 2. The endpaper map in George Ellis's *Gold Rush Desert Trails to San Diego and Los Angeles in 1849 (113)* is reproduced from the map in King's journal at the University of Arkansas.

King and several friends went into business and opened stores in Sonora, Santa Cruz, and San Francisco. A curious note: On March 2, 1850, he and fifteen associates formed the "Montazuma Secret Mining Associated Brethren," which was a pact promising never to reveal to anyone but themselves how much money they made in California.

King returned to Arkansas for a time, where he served two terms in the state legislature. He came back to California in 1886 and purchased the *Riverside Daily Enterprise,* and papers in Paso Robles and Santa Inez (*San Francisco Call,* 8/6/1897). He died in San Jose, California. [FS-ST-GT]

66. KING, ARTHUR

"Diary." Unknown location.

Arthur King was a member of the Fayetteville, Lincoln County (Tennessee) Company, which was captained by Robert Farquharson. A note in the *Lincoln County Tennessee Pioneers* (September 1976) suggests that King kept a diary in which he listed the names of his traveling companions. A number of individuals from the Fayetteville Company signed in at the Rancho Santa Ana del Chino indicating that they left Tennessee on April 14 and arrived in California on September 30, 1849. He was from Memphis, according to C. W. Haskins (1890:396). [FS-ST-GT]

67. LA GRANGE COMPANY

"The Journal of the La Grange Company: Being the Record of a Journey from Texas to California in 1849," edited by Carlo M. de Ferrari. *The Quarterly of the Tuolumne County Historical Society* 6 (Oct.–Dec. 1966):182–184; 6 (Jan.–March 1967): 193–200; 6 (April–June 1967):206–212; 7 (July–Sept. 1967): 217–220; 7 (Oct.–Dec. 1967):224–228; 7 (Jan.–Mar. 1968): 236–240. A handwritten copy of the entire document, cataloged under the name of John B. Cameron, is in the Department of Special Collections, Stanford University.

This journal enjoys the distinction of having three diarists, each of whom recorded segments of the journey. Entries by John Murchison *(69),* organizer of the wagon train, began on May 27 and ended on July 28, when he was accidentally killed by the discharge of his own rifle near the San Bernardino Rancho, Sonora. He had recorded the company's trip on Texas's Upper Emigrant Road between La Grange and Coons' Ranch, Texas. Comrade Samuel Birt *(22)* took over diary duties on August 1, 1949. His entries are detailed and include lively portraits of the people they met and the sites they visited between the San Bernardino Rancho and the Yuma Crossing. Birt left the company for reasons unknown. John B. Cameron *(28)*, the last of the trio, gamely took over the travelogue at Yuma until his arrival at Sullivan's Creek, California, on November 10, 1849, when he wrote: "pitcht our tents and unloded the wagons with two munths provetions and the nesery tools for mining, I will close the Jurnal by signing my name . . ." Then he tabulated the number of miles between Austin, Texas, and Sonora, California—2,477. The journal is interesting, well edited, and adds much that is new to the record. According to de Ferrari, the original document was owned by Leonard Rehm. Its location is not known.

68. MAY, JOHN, 1819–1854

"Correspondence, 1849–1851." Manuscript in the Special Collections Library, University of Arkansas, Fayetteville.

John May detailed his overland adventures with the Clarksville (Arkansas) Company in seven letters to his wife, Carolyn. In addition, there are sixteen letters describing his sojourn in California and his business venture with Alfred D. King as co-owner of stores in Santa Cruz, Sonora, and San Francisco. Because much of the material in the first portion of King's "Trip to the Gold Fields" *(65)* cannot be verified, May's story should help fill in the blanks. May returned to Clarksville, Arkansas. [FS-ST-GT]

69. MURCHISON, JOHN, ca. 1807–1849

"The Journal of the La Grange Company . . ." Refer to the La Grange Company entry *(67)* for full bibliographic citation and description of the trip.

John Murchison was one of three diarists who wrote about the experiences of the La Grange (Texas) Company. It has been said that more forty-niners were killed by accidental shots from their own guns than by Indians, and Murchison became one of those statistics. John B. Cameron *(28)* composed the following epitaph on September 12, which is preserved in the "Rancho Santa Ana del Chino Register Book" *(102)*:

"I regret to mention the death of Capt. John Murchison, one hundred & fifty miles west of the reor grand on the 27th day of July presisly at 12 oclock he was axidanchely shot by the discharg of his on gun being in the act of leeding his horse under the swinging lims of a tree his gun being swong in a Strap on the horn of the Sadle a well known custom of caring guns Some of the lims raking back the brich & lock throwing forward the musele in which position She was dischargd The ball entring a little under the right Sholder blade and coming out a little a bove the left brest. he fell & expired instonstaniousley with out a Strugal or the utrance of one Singal word he has lived respected and died regreted." [TT–ST]

70.   NOBLE, ROBERT WATSON, 1807–?

"Diary of a Journey from Chihuahua, Mexico to the Pueblo de San Jose, California, April 10–August 1, 1849." Manuscript (1849) in the Parkman Family Papers, Bancroft Library.

Samuel Parkman ran a number of mining ventures in Guanajuato, Mexico, and went into partnership with Noble, who drove sixty mules from Chihuahua to sell to California miners. Noble and fourteen trail hands traveled north to Janos, took up the Southern Trail at Guadalupe Pass, and moved on to California, passing Tucson and the Pima villages before arriving at the Yuma Crossing. Apparently he lost a good many of his animals, for on June 10 John Durivage *(42)* noted that Noble abandoned a wagon near Second Well, on which he left a "notice" in both English and Spanish saying he intended to return for his wagon and asking that it not be mutilated. Noble also left some information about the road and water sources. Durivage further said that "there is not a man who ever reads that paper that will ever cease to entertain the kindest feelings and the warmest gratitude to Robert Wilson [Watson] Noble ..." Noble suffered a good deal from heat and as he approached San Felipe Indian village on June 18, came upon a number of "dead bodies some lying by the side of their horses, also dead, with bridle in their hands."

Also included in the collection is a letter to Samuel Parkman from the Pueblo of San Jose giving an account of the trip.

An 1850 census of San Joaquin County listed Noble as a native of Connecticut and a merchant worth some $5,000 (CSJC 1959). [MX-ST-GT]

71.   NUGENT, JOHN, 1829–1880

"Scraps of Early History, IV." *The Argonaut,* Vol. 2, no.11, March 23, 1878.

Nugent describes his experiences as a member of John Coffee Hays's emigrating company and sets down some details of the first trip over the Apache Pass Trail. He tells us that J. G. Parke later surveyed the cutoff, naming it "Nugent's Wagon Road." We are treated to a number of lively vignettes including the details of their meeting with Mexican troops under leadership of General José María Elías. Most travelers had little to say about Tucson, but this traveler was enchanted with his stay in the presidio: "with its delicious nights out of doors, under the refulgent moon, listening in happy, dreamy lassitude to the untutored voices of the dark-eyed maidens, accompanying themselves on the guitar..." Nugent was one of five individuals who recorded the trip by Apache Pass.

Nugent was a San Leandro attorney and journalist. He was posthumously elected to the California Journalism Hall of Fame in 1959 (Thrapp 1988:1065). [TT-AP]

72.   PANCOAST, CHARLES EDWARD, 1818–1906

A Quaker Forty Niner, edited by Anna Paschall Hannum. Philadelphia: University of Pennsylvania Press, 1930.

Although he penned his narrative many years after the fact, the former Missouri River steamboat pilot appears to have total recall of the details of his trip. This pathfinder joined the Peoria (Illinois) Company and started for Santa Fe out of Fort Leavenworth, Kansas, on April 29, 1849. He tells us that at first he would not eat pork, but it was not long before he changed his mind: "all I wanted was enough" (p. 177). A highlight of the trip was his meeting with Kit Carson at his ranch in Rayado. He was "a superior representative of the genuine Rocky Mountain Hunter," Pancoast wrote, "his skin was dark and he wore his long black hair over his coat...He dressed in first class Indian style in Buckskin coat and pants trimmed with leather dangles, and wore moccasins on his feet and a Mexican Sombrero on his head" (p. 209). After a short stop in Santa Fe, Pancoast and his companions kept to the Southern Trail, arriving in the Mariposa region on February 15, 1850.

Pancoast had had enough of California by 1853, so returned to Philadelphia, where he went into real estate and entered politics. [SF-ST]

73.   PATTISON, GEORGE K.

"Journal," *Newark (N.J.) Morning Eagle*, April 3, 23; May 17, 23; June 2, 27; and November 20, 21, 1849.

Pattison outlines his daily activities in a series of interesting letters. He wrote that he was particularly impressed with the Rev. Americus L. Hay, a Baptist minister whom he met near North Fork Town in the Creek Nation on May 27. Here, Pattison described a prayer meeting that Hay conducted in the Creek language. Rumormongers were active in Santa Fe, where he arrived on July 28, sending forth discouraging reports about further travel. "In view of all," he said, "we shall proceed...thinking that California is still the richest country in gold upon the earth." I do not know of Pattison's fate since his last letter was written from Pecos, New Mexico. [FS-]

74.   PENNELL, WILLIAM DOYLE, 1814–?

"Letters of William Doyle and Delila Ann (Usher) Pennell, 1849–1852," William Doyle Pennell Collection, 1849–1885, California State Library, Sacramento. A typescript is in the Huntington Library.

Pennell wrote that he began his journey on May 23 at Council Grove, where he joined Colonel Congreave Jackson's Marion County (Missouri) Company. The men trod the Santa Fe Trail to Taos, where they took a brief respite to make a fruitless search for gold. He gives little detail about the route, but his list of people and companies he met along the way may be of interest. In an April 8, 1850, letter to his wife, he described how he met her former teacher, Mr. Howard, near the Gila River. Pennell added that he was present when Howard's wife gave birth to the first American child born in Arizona—a boy named Gila.

Pennell arrived safely and had some success mining in the Agua Fria area. [SF-ST-GT]

75.   PLATT, "SILENT"

The Diary of a Forty Niner, edited by Chauncy de Leon Canfield. Boston: Houghton Mifflin Company, 1920.

The diary is thought to have been written by Alfred T. Jackson of Norfolk, Connecticut. Platt's story appears on pages 132–136 and mirrors experiences of other forty-niners. He traveled across Texas roads and along the Southern Trail. The book is mainly an entertaining account of a miner's life. [TT-ST-GT]

76. POWELL, H. M. T.

The Santa Fe Trail to California, 1849–1852. The Journal and Drawings of H. M. T. Powell, edited by Douglas S. Watson. San Francisco: The Grabhorn Press, 1931. Sol Lewis, New York, reprinted the journal in a limited edition of 350 in 1981, with a new foreword by Howard Lamar. The original journal and sketchbook are in the Bancroft Library.

This has long been considered one of the better accounts of travel in 1849. And, in addition to recounting the overland experiences of the Illinois Company, Powell includes some remarkable sketches of the trail and California landmarks, one being an early view of the pueblo of Los Angeles. He writes that he and his companions left Greenville, Illinois, for Santa Fe on April 3, 1849, and continued on the Southern Trail by way of Galisteo and Abo, reaching San Diego on December 3, 1849. Powell went on to the mines by way of the California coast.

Though he is a bit of a complainer, Powell wrote vivid accounts of the trip and descriptions of the people and settlements encountered along the way. His journal has been of invaluable assistance in retracing and locating segments of the Southern Trail, especially in the Animas Valley area of New Mexico. The company was attempting to follow Philip St. George Cooke's directions *(104),* but on September 14, 1849, Powell wrote that "Cooke's topographical skill is poor; the main features are right so that we can tell pretty well where we are getting to, but it is a source of regret to me every day that some such a man as Emory was not with him." We learn that Powell was unable to find steady work in California, so worked at a number of odd jobs. He gave it all up in February 1852 and returned home. All efforts to trace later activities of the gentleman have failed. [SF-ST-GT]

77. POWNALL, JOSEPH, 1818–1890

"From Louisiana to Mariposa," edited by Robert Glass Cleland. *Pacific Historical Review* (February 1949):24–32. Pownall's journal and letter book are in the Huntington Library. The Pownall Family Papers (1857–1895) are in the Bancroft Library.

Pownall went across Texas by way of Dallas and to the Guadalupe Pass trailhead through Janos, Chihuahua, "which was a barren region having nothing to interest the traveler except the *Silver Mine*" (p. 26). He left Keachie, Louisiana, on March 28 and arrived at the Mariposa diggings on September 7, 1849.

After realizing some profit from mining, Pownall moved to Columbia, California, where he acquired an interest in the Tuolumne Water Company. He became superintendent in 1882 and was a member of the board of directors until his death (HTC 1882:343). [TM-ST-GT]

78. RAMSEY, W. WILBERFORCE A., 1825–1850

"W. Wilberforce A. Ramsey, Esq. and the California Gold Rush," by Thomas J. Noel. *Journal of the West* 12 (October 1973):563–575. The Ramsey letters are in the James G. Ramsey Papers, James D. Hoskins Library, University of Tennessee, Knoxville.

Wilberforce and his brother Alexander came from a prominent Tennessee family. Armed with letters of introduction and credit, they signed up with the East Tennessee Mining Company under the leadership of General Alexander Outlaw Anderson. The men got off to a late start on the Fort Smith–Santa Fe Trail and, as a result, decided to winter near Albuquerque. Apparently this group of bachelors was quite popular with the señoritas, and attendance at numerous fandangos kept the southerners entertained. Back on the trail again, they had trouble with General Anderson, who Ramsey described as dishonest and incapable of properly managing the company, thus prolonging the journey unnecessarily.

Anderson apparently was oblivious to all of this when he wrote of their safe arrival in the "Rancho Santa Ana del Chino Register Book" *(102)* on April 18, 1850. He said that "his" men were well disciplined and well armed, and that they had not had even one day of suffering. He neglected to add their names to the "Register."

Finally, a sad letter written by friend and companion David A. Deaderick on November 20, 1850 *(40)*, told about Wilberforce Ramsey's last illness and death. [FS-ST-GT]

79. RANDALL, ANDREW, ca. 1816–1856

"Diary of Dr. Andrew Randall, April 19, 1849–August 19, 1849." Manuscript (1849) in California State Library.

Randall had worked for the *Minnesota Register* before joining the James Collier contingent (*33*:12), which followed the Cimarron Cutoff to Santa Fe, where he made his last diary entry on August 19. In addition to numerous geological descriptions, Randall provides a superb description of Santa Fe, though critical, since he wrote that many of the army officers enjoyed the exotic enticements of that town more than he thought they should.

A second half of the diary has not been located, but we know Randall continued to travel with Collier since both Edward Beckwith *(20)* and William Brisbane *(26)* mention his presence. Randall arrived safely in California, where he soon enriched himself by selling real estate. He was respected and loved by all his neighbors in Marin County—except one Joseph Hetherington, to whom he owed money. On July 26, 1856, Hetherington walked up to Randall in the St. Nicholas Hotel in San Francisco and gunned him down. The vigilance committee took charge of Hetherington, tried him, found him guilty, and hanged him three days later (Bancroft 1887:489 500). [SF-ZU-GT]

80.   RICKS, CASPAR STINEMETS

"Caspar Stinemets Diary," typed transcript (carbon), June 26–Aug 10, 1849 in the Bancroft Library. "Diary, 1849 and records, 1861–1863." Manuscript in Holt-Atherton Department of Special Collections, University of the Pacific Libraries, Stockton, California, attributed to D. Lambert Fouts *(49)*.

Owen Coy quoted extensively from this diary in *The Great Trek (107)* and attributed authorship to Caspar Stinemets Ricks, founder of the city of Eureka, California. It has been shown that Ricks was not the author of the diary (see Fouts, *49*). Moreover, there is little evidence to show that D. Lambert Fouts wrote the work either.

Nevertheless, that does not diminish the importance of this very interesting diary, since it contains excellent coverage of the journey between Albuquerque and Santa Cruz, Sonora. The typescript in the Bancroft Library has been compared with the original at the University of the Pacific and is an accurate transcription. Provenance of the typescript cannot be determined.

The California State Library holds the *Biography and Diary of Caspar Stinemets Ricks,* n.p., n.d. This diary was written by the real Caspar Stinemets Ricks (1821–1888) between April and August 1862 while on a trip in Humboldt County, and bears no relationship to the two versions mentioned above. As noted in the Fouts entry, Ricks arrived in San Francisco on August 18, 1849, by way of Panama. There is a master's thesis about the man: "The Forgotten Pioneer—the Story of C. S. Ricks," by Tim Springer, Humboldt State University.

81. ROBB, JOHN S. "SOLITAIRE," 1815–1856

"Gold Fever: The Letters of 'Solitaire,' Goldrush Correspondent of '49," edited by John Francis McDermott. *Missouri Historical Society Bulletin* 5(January 1949):115–126; 5(April 1949):211–223; 5(July 1949):316-331; 6(October 1949): 33–43.

Writing as "Solitaire," Robb supplied the *St. Louis Weekly Reveille* with lengthy letters from New Orleans, Corpus Christi, San Diego, and the Sonora mining district that recounted vignettes about his cross-country trek and life in the mines. A wagon or pack trip to California in 1849 was no joy ride, and Robb seemed to suffer more than most from lack of water. At the same time, he lost most of his animals due to heat and exhaustion.

Robb was destined to stay in the publishing business and is noted for bringing the first printing presses to California *(San Francisco Alta California, 2/6/1850)*. He edited both the *Stockton Journal* and *Sacramento Age* (Kemble 1962:159, 372) until his premature death in 1856. He was buried in Sacramento (*Alta California,* 10/7/1856).

82. SHINN, SILAS MONROE, 1821–?

The Trail of a Pioneer, Auburn, Calif.: Press of Placer County Republican, [1910?].

Shinn, from Russellville, Arkansas, recalls his trip to California on the Fort Smith–Santa Fe and Southern trails. The rare, privately published booklet is in the California State Library. He left Fort Smith early in April 1849, and hooked up with the Southern Trail near Albuquerque, New Mexico. He continued on to San Diego, where he found passage to Sacramento, arriving the following November. His reminiscences are skimpy except for sections on his encounters with Indians and lengthy passages of religious moralizing. He apparently stayed in California and over the next sixty years returned twice to Arkansas to visit his wife. [FS-ST-GT]

83.   SIMMONS, JOSEPH R.

"Diary, 1849–1850," in the Joint Collection, University of Missouri Western Historical Manuscript Collection—Columbia and State Historical Society of Missouri Manuscripts.

Here are two volumes, each containing stories of the same overland trip. A small leather boundbook of eighty-nine pages was likely the volume in which Simmons kept the daily notes of his experiences. The second volume was obviously written at a later date (the flyleaf reads: "From an old Diary of J. R. S.") and is an expanded version of the original.

Simmons left Westport, Missouri, on May 29, 1849, with a company under the leadership of former Governor John C. Edwards. It followed the Santa Fe and Southern trails and arrived in Agua Fria in the Mariposa mining region on February 28, 1850. This traveler recorded both mileage and daily events and left a good description of the various towns they passed. He tells us how he built a raft to go fishing on the Gila, then used it to transport the company's supplies. Except for some unplanned landings on sand bars, he wrote that he and his friends sailed their boat all the way to the Yuma Crossing. His account of the journey between Los Angeles and Mariposa is particularly well done. Simmons disappears from the record at this point. [SF-ST-GT]

84.   SNIFFEN, GEORGE S.

"Notes by the Camp Fire; Being a Narrative of an Overland Journey from the United States to California in the Year 1849." John B. Goodman Collection, Manuscript 26, Mandeville Special Collections Library, University of California, San Diego.

George Sniffen was elected treasurer for the Havilah Mining Company from New York. In addition to keeping the books, he also kept track of travel, noting that the company spent 260 days to cover 4,497 miles. The men were on the Fort Smith–Santa Fe Trail by April 23, 1849. Sniffen described San Miguel del Vado, collected pottery shards at Pecos, and made a stop at Galisteo before joining the Southern Trail near Garfield. His diary comes in handy to compare with those of his traveling companions, Woolsey Teller (89) and George Pattison (73), both of whom stopped writing near Pecos, New Mexico. [FS-ST-GT]

85. STEVENS, BENJAMIN, 1801–1896

Untitled manuscript (1849) in the John Lewis RoBards Papers, Joint Collection, University of Misssouri Western Historical Manuscript Collection—Columbia and State Historical Society of Missouri Manuscripts.

The first few pages of the journal are missing, but according to David P. Robrock, editor of the William W. Hunter journal, internal evidence suggests that Benjamin Stevens, a Baptist minister, was its author (*62*:286). This is a fine work from which to study details of the trip and learn something about the various travelers whose names are liberally sprinkled throughout. The group started out from Hannibal, Missouri, took the Santa Fe Trail, and bypassed the capital by taking the Galisteo road to the Rio Grande. Continuing on the Southern Trail, they arrived at the Colorado River on October 30. An unusual number of emigrants in this train died from accidental gunshot wounds, one from a stabbing, and several from cholera. Stevens was kept busy conducting services for all and now and then doubted if he would ever make it to California. He was another who enjoyed the distinction of sailing down the Gila River with the parents of Gila Howard, the first American child born in Arizona. [SF-ST-GT]

86. STRENTZEL, JOHN T., ca. 1813–1890

"Life of Dr. John T. Strentzel," *Chronicles of the Builders of the Commonwealth,* by Hubert Howe Bancroft. Vol. 3:435–444. Ten-page typescript (1890) in the Bancroft Library. A longer holograph version is also in the Bancroft Library.

In addition to writing about his life in Europe and sojourn in Texas, Strentzel tells about his 1849 trip to California. We learn that he left Dallas, Texas, on March 29, 1849, with a company of 135, including 25 children and 9 women. He recalls ninety days of rough travel on a route that went west from Waco, past Monahans Sandhills and the Guadalupe Mountains (Texas), ending at Coons' Ranch. After a welcome rest, they moved north along the Rio Grande to pick up the Southern Trail near Garfield. Strentzel settled in Contra Costa County, where he established the successful Alhambra Vineyards. [TT-ST-GT]

87. STRENTZEL, LOUISIANA, 1821–1897

"A Letter from California, 1849," edited by Kenneth L.

Holmes. Vol. 1, *Covered Wagon Women, Diaries and Letters from the Western Trails 1840–1890*. Glendale, Calif.: The Arthur H. Clark Company, 1983. Pp. 247–269. Typescript of letter is in the Strentzel Family Papers (1842–1964) in the Bancroft Library. The original document is in a private collection.

Wife of John Strentzel, Louisiana is one of two women known to have detailed a journey on the Southern Trail (see *37*). She described her adventures in a letter to her parents, written soon after her arrival in San Diego, California. Among her interesting stories is one relating to the death of former President James Polk. The company heard about it while in camp on the Gila. Louisiana tells how emigrants began to withdraw to their tents and a few moments later, returned in mourning clothes if they had them.

In spite of the rigors of the trip, she mentions that she and her children had never been in better health. One day her daughter Louie would marry the famed naturalist and writer John Muir. [TT-ST-GT]

88.   STUART, JACOB

"The Diary of a '49-er'—Jacob Stuart," by Miss Kate White. *Tennessee Historical Magazine* 1 (July 1931):279–285.

Jacob Stuart left St. Joseph on July 20 with the East Tennessee Mining Company, headed by General Alexander Outlaw Anderson. According to the "Register Book," they arrived at the Rancho Santa Ana del Chino on April 18, 1850 *(102)*. This work includes a number of letters which were dated to 1850 instead of 1849, thus causing some confusion in defining the sojourn in Albuquerque. The men left St. Joseph on July 20, arrived in Albuquerque in November, and were in California by April 1850. The Ramsey *(78)* article puts a better perspective on this badly edited effort. [SF-ST-GT]

89.   TELLER, WOOLSEY

"The Santa Fe Trail to California. The Letters of Woolsey Teller. Written on the Trail and in California in Description of His Trip Across the Plains and in the New Eldorado, 1849-50." Manuscript in the Yale Collection of Western Americana, Beinecke Rare Book and Manuscript Library.

Like traveling companion George Pattison *(73)*, Teller stopped writing in Santa Fe. His letters to his brother add new material, however, and he describes a Choctaw ball game and paints an interesting picture of James Edwards and his settlement near Little River in Indian Territory, Oklahoma. He admitted that he had never seen a Mexican before and found them "objects of curiosity." Teller left New York on March 19, arriving in San Diego on December 2, 1849. Letters written from San Francisco in 1850 describe life in the city and his plans to import scarce articles of food and open a restaurant. [FS-ST-GT]

90. THIBAULT, FREDERICK JAMES, 1820–1874

"Letter," *Little Rock Arkansas State Gazette & Democrat,* April 19, 1850; "Excerpts From the Journal of F. J. Thibault," *Little Rock Arkansas State Gazette & Democrat,* January 31, July 11, and May 9, 1851.

Thibault traveled with the Little Rock Company and provided some colorful accounts of the group's experiences on Guadalupe Pass and with the Yuma Indians at the Colorado Crossing. The final excerpt details his return to Arkansas via Nicaragua, Panama, and Cuba. His original journal has not been located.

Some time later, he returned to California with his family and went to work for J. Biedelman's mercantile company before settling down to a successful career as notary public, "evidenced by the fact that for many years his fees were much larger than any other notary" *(San Francisco Alta California,* 11/26/1874). [FS-ST-GT]

91. WEED, L. N.

"Narrative of a Journey to California in 1849." Manuscript (1857) in the Yale Collection of Western Americana, Beinecke Rare Book and Manuscript Library.

We learn that Weed sailed out of New York on the bark *Norumbega* on March 8, 1849. After landing in Galveston, he made his way to Austin and Fredericksburg, then to Coons' Ranch and El Paso del Norte on the Upper Emigrant Road, leaving a fairly good report of conditions in Texas towns. Weed was a people watcher and forthright in expressing his cultural biases. As a matter of fact, when describing the natives—Indians or Mexicans—he invariably included a remark about the depth of their skin color. He said that Mexican women valued lighter skin color and that on one occasion the proprietress of a store in a small town suggested he marry her daughter: "but as I had not intended to commit matrimony I declined" (p. 23). In addition to detailing his adventures on the Southern Trail, Weed describes his trip to the southern mining region and his life there. He returned to New York in December 1850. [TT-ST-GT]

92.   WILLIAMS, R. G.

"Letters from the California Adventurers," *Knoxville (Tenn.) Register,* August 18 and 25, September 22, and December 29, 1849; January 5 and June 6, 1850.

Williams recorded the trip of the East Tennessee Mining Company, which was led by Alexander Outlaw Anderson. As noted by David Deaderick *(40),* Jacob Stuart *(88),* and Wilberforce Ramsey *(78)* this company got off to a late start and spent some time in Santa Fe and Albuquerque before making the final push to California. The last letter in this group was written from Las Vegas, New Mexico. The men arrived at the Rancho Santa Ana del Chino on April 18, 1850 *(102).* [SF-ST-GT]

93.   WOOD, HARVEY, 1828–1895

Personal Recollections, edited by John B. Goodman. Pasadena, Calif.: Grant Dahlstrom, 1955. Two hundred copies were reprinted from a pamphlet produced in 1896 by the Mountain Echo Job Printing Office at Angel's Camp, California.

Harvey Wood wrote his memoirs in 1878 from his home in Angel's Camp, California, where he had been running Robinson's Ferry since 1856. He recalled sailing from New York on February 13, 1849, in company with members of the Kit Carson Association. After arrival in Corpus Christi, he continued overland to Laredo. Instead of taking the road by Monterrey and Saltillo, Wood and his companions risked a 500-mile, hazardous shortcut over a barren area between Monclova and Saucillo, then turned north to connect with the Guadalupe Pass road. On the way, they stopped for sightseeing in Chihuahua. Continuing on the Southern Trail, he and his companions were among the early arrivals in the southern mines and were hard at work in July. [TM-ST-GT]

94.   WOODRUFF, ALDEN M., 1830–?

"Letters," *Little Rock Arkansas State Democrat,* June 1,

August 17, December 21, 1849, and January 25, 1850; *Little Rock Arkansas State Gazette & Democrat*, April 19 and 26, and October 11, 1850.

Here are some colorful letters from the son of the editor of the *Arkansas Gazette*. In addition to vignettes of travel with the Little Rock Company, he reported some sad tales about his mining ventures at Indian Bar on the Tuolumne River. He returned to Little Rock in 1851 to edit the *Little Rock Arkansas Gazette* (10/10/1851). His new position was apparently short-lived, for he soon disappeared from the record (Ross 1984). [FS-ST-GT]

95. WOZENCRAFT, OLIVER M., 1814–1887

"Through Northern Mexico in '49," *California and Overland Monthly* 6 (1882):421–428.

Dr. Wozencraft dramatized his experiences on the way to California, emphasizing the Mexican portion of his journey. He sailed from New Orleans in February 1849 to Brownsville, Texas. After crossing the Rio Grande to Mexico, he followed the Chihuahua road north to Guadalupe Pass. His story ends at the Colorado Crossing with a description of the desert mirage.

It was about this time that Wozencraft conceived the idea of irrigating the desert near Calexico with the waters of the Colorado, and so devoted his life to making it a reality. As a result, histories credit him as being the father of California's Imperial Valley. He was also a member of the state's first constitutional convention. Many years later, he helped Theodore Judah advocate the building of a transcontinental railway. Wozencraft ultimately settled in San Bernardino (Ingersoll 1904:686). [MX-ST-GT]

SOUTHERN AND GILA TRAILS
REFERENCE WORKS

Following is a list of books and articles that provide useful background material about the development, exploration, and research of Southern Route travel. It is not exhaustive since I have selected only those books that I consider the best for further study of a particular area. Depending on focus, a dedicated researcher might want to consult Mormon Battalion diaries, books on the Santa Fe Trail, the Butterfield Overland Mail, and more.

96. ABERT, JAMES W.

Through the Country of the Comanche Indians in the Fall of the Year 1845. The Journal of a U.S. Army Expedition Led by Lieutenant James W. Abert of the Topographical Engineers, edited by John Galvin. San Francisco: Howell Books, 1970.

   Abert's book is particularly useful for locating sites along the Fort Smith–Santa Fe Trail that are located in west Texas and New Mexico. Colonel John James Abert, chief of the Corps of Topographical Engineers, assigned his son James to the first independent command to survey south and east along the Canadian River in west Texas and the Llano Escatado area of eastern New Mexico.

97. BARTLETT, JOHN RUSSELL

Personal Narrative of Explorations and Incidents in Texas, New Mexico, California, Sonora, and Chihuahua, etc. Two volumes. New York: D. Appleton & Company, 1854.

   Bartlett was commissioner of the United States and Mexican boundary survey and crossed and recrossed the forty-niners' road a number of times between 1850 and 1853. His tenure as commissioner was clouded by financial problems and bickering by personnel. However, before he was suspended, he managed to write a classic story of travel, history, and drama in the western desert. His observations and excellent sketches help clarify and fill gaps in the emigrants' stories of travel on the Southern Trail, particularly in southern Arizona and New Mexico.

98. BENDER, A. B.

"Opening Routes Across West Texas, 1848–1850," *Southwestern Historical Quarterly* 27 (October 1933):116–135.

Bender provided historical background and details of the federal government's program for exploration and survey of routes through Texas following the Mexican War. New roads helped link towns on the western frontier—Fredericksburg, Austin, and San Antonio—with sites in the Rio Grande valley and were heavily used by emigrants as they funneled into southern trails. Bender gives us a map outlining eleven different trails that were opened between 1848 and 1850. (see also *124*).

99. BERRY, ROBERT L., EDITOR AND JAMES A. BIER,

CARTOGRAPHER

Western Emigrant Trails, 1830–1870, second edition, Independence, Mo: Oregon-California Trails Association, 1993.

Though most maps accompanying the various sources listed here are critiqued, students of trails are encouraged to consult this edition. In the past, National Geographic, American Heritage, and other publishing houses have produced hundreds of maps defining the various trails. These are not recommended except for historic reasons since new and continued on-site research has in many cases changed trail names and their configuration. Contributors to the Western Emigrant Trails map were sought out because of their expertise on the numerous segments represented. As a result, for the first time we have an accurate rendition of all of the major trails used by emigrants between 1830 and 1860.

100. BIEBER, RALPH P., EDITOR

Southern Trails to California in 1849, Vol. 5. Southwestern Historical Series. Glendale, Calif.: The Arthur H. Clark Company, 1937.

In addition to reprinting the journals of John E. Durivage *(42)*, Augustus M. Heslep *(56)*, and an anonymous goldseeker *(16)*, Bieber references numerous letters written by forty-niners en route to California on one of the southern trails. At the same time, he provides a descriptive history of the various routes. He also includes a map, which is incredibly accurate given the small amount of information available to him at the time. As a matter of fact, others tried to improve upon the map Bieber included and began to perpetuate numerous mistakes over time. As a result, most maps published since then should be viewed with some skepticism.

101. BROWN, WILLIAM E.
The Santa Fe Trail. St. Louis, Mo.: The Patrice Press, 1990.

This republication of the 1963 limited edition will provide valuable assistance in studying the route and general history of the Santa Fe Trail. There are two parts: the first contains an overall history of the trail; the second contains a report on site conditions contrasted with first-hand accounts of early travelers. Records show that a minority of travelers out of Independence, Missouri, followed the Santa Fe Trail in order to connect with either the Southern or Gila trails during 1849. The Santa Fe Trail had been the main cultural and commercial link between New Mexico and the United States for over 100 years, and stories of travel across the vast prairies and contacts with numerous American Indian tribes and the New Mexicans stirred imaginations. There are hundreds of books available for an in-depth study of the trail. However, in addition to the forty-niner stories listed in this work, readers should consult a diary kept by an eighteen-year-old bride, Susan Shelby Magoffin, between 1846 and 1847, *Down the Santa Fe Trail and into Mexico* (University of Nebraska Press, 1962). It is considered to be one of the finest journals kept by a nineteenth-century American woman. In 1987, Congress designated the Santa Fe Trail National Historic Trail under the National Trails System Act. The non-profit Santa Fe Trails Association, headquartered in Larned, Kansas, is dedicated to promoting public awareness and appreciation of the historic trail, which until 1846 terminated in Mexico.

102. BYNUM, LINDLEY, EDITOR
"Record Book of the Rancho Santa Ana del Chino," *Historical Society of Southern California* 16 (1934):1–55. The original manuscript, "Rancho Santa Ana del Chino Register Book," is in the Huntington Library.

A number of emigrants turned west to San Diego after reaching Warner's Ranch, California, then proceeded to San Francisco by ship from San Diego. But those who continued on foot invariably passed Isaac Williams's Rancho Santa Ana del Chino, located about thirty miles east of Los Angeles. Williams received a grant to the Chino Ranch in 1841 after his marriage into the Lugo family. It was not long before the ranch prospered. He kept his door open and was both hospitable and generous to those who passed by. This is particularly true during the days of '49, when hundreds of argonauts straggled by his house.

William Goulding, whose diary is listed here was among the first arrivals, and he and Williams became friends. On August 12 he wrote that he "found Mr. Williams to be an open-hearted and frank American and expressed all he said with his mouth, with his eye, and with his hands too for he instantly assisted us in unsaddling our packed mules . . ." (51). It was probably Goulding who urged Williams to ask those who passed by to leave their names and/or a short report in the register, since the heading was in Goulding's handwriting as was the first message dated August 12. Not all who passed left their names. But those who did praised Williams, or told of hardships on the trail, inserted notes for friends yet to arrive, and even described lost animals. The leader of a company very often wrote down the names of his fellow travelers.

We can learn a great deal about the southern migration by studying the document. For example, out of 570 names added between August 12, 1849 and June 5, 1850, 80 percent represented twelve southern states, with the majority coming from Arkansas and Texas. Emigrants from ten northern states, particularly New York, comprised the remaining 20 percent. Those that can be further identified formed into forty companies for protection during the journey. These travelers told stories from travel on the Gila, Southern, and Apache Pass trails. In addition, a large contingent came to the ranch from the Old Spanish Trail out of Salt Lake (Etter 1990). Not included in this study were names added sporadically through 1856.

103. CONKLING, ROSCOE P. AND MARGARET B. CONKLING

The Butterfield Overland Mail, 1857–1869: Its organization and operation over the Southern Route to 1861; subsequently over the Central Route to 1866; and under Wells, Fargo and Company in 1869. 3 volumes. Glendale, Calif.: The Arthur H. Clark Company, 1947.

Long considered the definitive work on the Butterfield Stage, the volumes are essential reading since the stage route utilized hundreds of miles of forty-niner trails between California and Fort Smith, Arkansas. It is particularly helpful in locating segments of the Southern Trail on the Gila River between Maricopa Wells and Yuma, Arizona, and locations in New Mexico, especially through Cooke's Canyon. It includes maps, sketches, and photographs in addition to descriptions of the various sites where emigrants stopped to rest.

104. COOKE, PHILIP ST. GEORGE

Journal of the March of the Mormon Battalion. Senate Document 31, Special Session, 1849. Washington, D.C. Reprinted in *Exploring Southwest Trails,* edited by Ralph P. Bieber. Vol. 7, Southwest Historical Series. Glendale, Calif.: The Arthur H. Clark Company, 1938. *The Conquest of New Mexico and California.* New York: G. P. Putnam's Sons, 1878.

Cooke left Santa Fe on October 19, 1846, under orders from General Stephen Watts Kearny to assume control of the Mormon Battalion and open a wagon road to the Pacific. The oncoming forty-niners would follow Cooke's road (Southern Trail) as far as the San Pedro River near the Arizona-Sonora border. In addition to this report, numerous members of the Mormon Battalion left accounts of the trip. Sergeant Daniel Tyler's book *(131)* is particularly recommended and adds perspective from the Mormon point of view. The Senate version is Cooke's report of the trip. Later, Cooke rewrote his journal to produce *Conquest*, which he hoped would be both readable by the general public and informative at the same time.

105. COUCHMAN, DONALD HOWARD

Cooke's Peak—Pasaron Por Aqui: A Focus on United States History in Southwestern New Mexico. Las Cruces, N.Mex.: Bureau of Land Management, 1990.

Virtually every traveler on the Southern Trail stopped to water at Cooke's Springs, located on a narrow and rugged road that meanders through Cooke's Canyon north of Deming, New Mexico. Couchman sees the area as a focal point around which the consummation of U.S. Manifest Destiny pivoted, and this road a link between the East and the

West. The Indians, Spanish, and Mexicans passed here; the Mormon Battalion, emigrants of 1849, Commissioner John R. Bartlett, and the Butterfield Stage all helped to deepen the ribbon of road. Couchman provides tables, maps, and numerous illustrations to make this an important addition to Southern Route history.

106. COUTS, CAVE JOHNSON

Hepah! California! The Journal of Cave Johnson Couts from Monterrey, Nuevo Leon, Mexico to Los Angeles, California During the Years 1848–1849, edited by Henry F. Dobyns. Tucson, Ariz.: Arizona Pioneers' Historical Society, 1961. *From San Diego to the Colorado in 1849: The Journal and Maps of Cave J. Couts,* edited by William McPherson. Los Angeles: Arthur M. Ellis, 1932. Manuscript copies are in both the Bancroft and Huntington libraries.

Cave Couts was a lieutenant in the U.S. Army assigned to occupation duty in Monterrey, Mexico, when he received orders to march to the Pacific under the command of Major Lawrence P. Graham to strengthen U.S. garrisons in upper California. Graham led his dragoons north to the Guadalupe Pass trailhead. They did not follow the San Pedro River as Cooke did, but continued to Santa Cruz, Sonora, and turned north to Tucson by way of the Santa Cruz Valley. Emigrants of 1849 subsequently chose the route (which sometimes was called Graham's Road). Couts wrote that the men left Monterrey, Nuevo Leon on June 27, 1848, and arrived at the Colorado Crossing on November 24, 1848. Couts had plenty to say about Graham's leadership, of which he heartily disapproved, and included colorful descriptions of his travels and the people he met along the way.

Couts compiled his second journal in 1849. This time, he was in charge of the military escort for Lieutenant Amiel Weeks Whipple's survey of the United States–Mexican boundary and camped near the Colorado River. In recording his experiences, Couts describes the condition of emigrants coming off the trail as they entered California in mid-September. He complains bitterly about being bombarded with their tales of woe at his various camps in the California desert. Nevertheless, he furnished extra rations to needy travelers.

107. COY, OWEN C.

The Great Trek. Los Angeles: The Powell Publishing Co.,
1929.

Coy's book covers the full gamut of overland experiences by providing
information on the Santa Fe, Oregon, and California trails; trails
through Mexico and Texas; something on the Death Valley crowd; and
the Salt Lake to Los Angeles Trail.

He has titled chapter 10 in this book "The Gila Trail," and quotes
extensively from the diaries of Judge Benjamin Hayes *(54)*, Cornelius
Cox *(36)*, and the Caspar S. Ricks/D. Lambert Fouts diaries *(80, 49)* to
chronicle the adventures of goldseekers on the Southern and lower Gila
trails. Coy also provides a bibliography that covers a broad area of overland journeys.

108. CREUZBAUR, ROBERT

Guide to California and the Pacific Ocean. New York: H. Long
& Brothers, 1849.

Though it bears a date of 1849, this book probably was not available
to overlanders until the latter part of the year. In addition to using the
records of the General Land Office of the state of Texas, Creuzbaur
draws from the reports of Cooke *(104)* and Emory *(114)* and John S.
Ford's map from Austin to Cooke's road (March, April, May, 1849). The
small forty-page booklet would handily fit into a pioneer's pocket and
contains a description of the various routes through the lower Mississippi Valley, Texas, and Mexico that connected with one of the trails to
California. Fold-out maps were tucked in the inside cover. Creuzbaur
also added some nineteenth-century travel tips for emigrants. Though
one can see the western United States and Mexico at a glance, it is not
likely that this map would have been of much help to the traveler. Moreover, emigrants on the Southern Trail followed the Santa Cruz River to
Tucson; Creuzbaur has them on the San Pedro. A Creuzbaur map was
used to illustrate Lorenzo Aldrich's journal.

109. CROUCH, BRODIE

Jornada del Muerto: A Pageant of the Desert. Vol. 15, The
Western Lands and Waters Series. Spokane, Wash.: The
Arthur H. Clark Company, 1989.

In addition to chronicling travel on the ninety-mile waterless jornada between San Marcial and San Diego Mound, New Mexico, the author gives a fine historical overview of an area that Indians, Spaniards, Mexicans, law men, bad men, and explorers had used for centuries. The jornada, of course, was part of the famed El Camino Real, which connected Santa Fe and Mexico City.

110. DISTURNELL, JOHN

The Emigrant's Guide to New Mexico, California, and Oregon; giving the Different Overland and Sea Routes. Compiled from Reliable Authorities with a Map. New York: J. Disturnell, 1849.

This may not have been available early in 1849, but it would have been the best guide for routes through Mexico. It was not totally accurate, but it did give travelers a reasonably good idea of what to expect. Like modern AAA guides, it attempted to describe the scenery and included the cost of food, lodging, mules, and stagecoach fares.

111. EDWARDS, E. I.

Lost Oasis Along the Carrizo. Los Angeles: Westernlore Press, 1961.

Edwards has carefully traced the emigrant trail from the Colorado Crossing near Yuma, Arizona, through Anza Borrego Desert State Park in California. At the same time, he provides an extensive bibliography that covers the history of travel in the area. He also furnishes a fine map for reference.

112. ELÍAS, JOSÉ MARÍA

"Jornadas," *Noticias estadisticas del estado de Sonora,* José Francisco Velasco. Mexico, 1850. A later publication is *Noticias Estadías del Estado de Sonora.* Hermosillo: Gobierno del Estado de Sonora, 1985. A microfilm copy of the campaign diary can be found at the Arizona Historical Society, Tucson: *The Campaign Diary of the Commanding General of Sonora, Don Jose Maria Elias Gonzales While Pursuing Wild Indians, September and October 1849,* compiled by Teodoro

Lopez de Aros. Translation by Diana Hadley and Dr. James Officer, University of Arizona.

General Elías and his Mexican troops were out in force to round up Apache Indians, and a number of diarists listed here reported meetings with him as he moved between Arizona and New Mexico along segments of the Southern Trail. These included: John Nugent (*71*); William Hunter (*62*); David Demarest (*41*); Charles Pancoast (*72*); and Robert Eccleston (*45*). Demarest described a meeting that took place on October 15 between Elías and John Coffee Hays (*55*) near Ben Moore Mountain. He said he counted 420 soldiers, who had collected two scalps, six ears, and three Apache prisoners. At the same time, he wrote that Elías provided Hays with a couple of guides to help him chart a direct route to Tucson, thus avoiding the longer road by Guadalupe Pass. The soldiers then left for Janos, Chihuahua.

113. ELLIS, GEORGE M., EDITOR

Gold Rush Desert Trails to San Diego and Los Angeles in 1849. San Diego, Calif.: Corral of the Westerners, 1995.

In addition to reassessing the significance of the Southern Route to California in 1849, the book features newly edited extracts from journals and/or diaries by nine individuals listed here who traveled between the Yuma Crossing and San Diego or Los Angeles. These are: Lorenzo D. Aldrich *(14);* John W. Audubon (*18*); Jacob H. Bachman (*19*); William H. Chamberlin (*5*); Cave J. Couts (*106*); David D. Demarest (*41*); John E. Durivage (*42*); H. M. T. Powell (*76*); and L. N. Weed (*91*). A second section includes a newly annotated version of the W. C. S. Smith journey up Baja (*166*) and the experiences of those who risked travel on the *San Blasena* (*181*). Section 3 contains articles on the Couts-Whipple wagon road and historic locations related to it. Also included are modern and historic maps, drawings, and reproductions of some Audubon paintings.

An unfortunate mix-up resulted in the endpaper map being attributed to Cave Couts from his diaries in the Bancroft Library. The map, which shows the route from the Yuma Crossing to Los Angeles, was drawn in 1849 by Alfred D. King (*65*) of the Clarksville (Arkansas) Company, and is with his papers in the Special Collections Library, University of Arkansas, Fayetteville. It is well known that Couts drew a number of "waybill" maps to help emigrants find their way, and Ellis (1996) believes that King copied his map from one of these.

114. EMORY, WILLIAM HEMSLEY

Notes of a Military Reconnaissance from Fort Leavenworth, in Missouri, to San Diego in California. Thirtieth Congress, First Session. Ex. Doc. No. 41; and Thirtieth Congress, First Session, Senate, Executive No. 7, Washington, D. C., 1848.

Lieutenant William H. Emory was assigned to General Stephen Watts Kearny's Army of the West in 1846, under orders to take possession of New Mexico and California. Emory's *Notes*, published in 1848, became an important guide for emigrants in the rush of 1849, since it detailed the trip along the Gila Trail, which left the Rio Grande at Truth or Consequences, New Mexico, and followed the course of the Gila River to the Yuma Crossing. He also mapped the route of the Mormon Battalion over the Southern Trail and along the San Pedro River to Tucson and to the Gila Trail at the Pima villages. *Notes* provided goldseekers with valuable information by discussing various Indian groups, thus allaying fears about tribes the pioneers might meet along the way. Since Emory's map is not to scale and covers hundreds of miles, one can not help but wonder how any one made it to California using it. Nevertheless, it appears that the majority of emigrants had both Emory's book and map with them, and they all found their way by connecting with the various landmarks Emory so gracefully described.

115. ETTER, PATRICIA A.

"To California on the Southern Route–1849," *Overland Journal* 13 (1995):2-14. "The Southern Route–1849 Journals: A Bibliography," *Bulletin of Bibliography* 43 (September 1986):131–148.

The article contains a brief overview and history of the three trails comprising the Southern Route: the Gila, Southern, and Apache Pass trails. The bibliography was an early attempt to list all known overland diaries, and some of those entries have been adapted for this work. A map shows the various trails including those in Mexico.

116. FOREMAN, GRANT

Marcy and the Goldseekers: The Journal of Captain R. B. Marcy, with an Account of the Gold Rush Over the Southern Route. Norman: University of Oklahoma Press, 1939. Second printing, 1968.

This volume contains Marcy's original report of his survey of the route to Santa Fe and his account of all that transpired as he escorted thousands of emigrants. In addition, Foreman has reproduced rare newspaper accounts and letters to recreate the history and drama of the first migration over the Fort Smith–Santa Fe Trail. It has become a classic and is essential to a study of 1849 westward migration. One caution: His map tracing the Southern Trail is inaccurate. Emigrants came down the west side of the Rio Grande (not over the Jornada del Muerto, as pictured); they followed the Santa Cruz River to Tucson (not the route Cooke took up the San Pedro); and dipped into Mexico after crossing the Colorado River (not over the Algodones Dunes in California, as pictured).

117. GREGG, JOSIAH

Commerce of the Prairies: Or the Journal of a Santa Fe Trader During Eight Expeditions Across the Great Western Prairies, and Residence of Nearly Nine Years in Northern Mexico. Two volumes. New York: Henry G. Langley, 1844. There have been numerous editions, but Max L. Moorehead's reprint with meticulous notes is still the best (University of Oklahoma Press, 1954, 1958, 1974, 1990).

Josiah Gregg was a veritable renaissance man of the prairies. He had studied both medicine and law, and was a mathematician, an amateur naturalist, and a keen observer. He was also an experienced frontiersman and professional trader, having crossed the plains eight times between 1831 and 1840. It was during his last expedition that he opened a trail between Van Buren, Arkansas, and Santa Fe, New Mexico. A segment of Gregg's path skirted the north side of the Canadian River, and a number of forty-niners started out this way before crossing the river at Choteau's Fort, Oklahoma, to join the Marcy road. The book is included here because it was read by the prospective goldseeker, eager to know more about upcoming adventures. Gregg not only writes about Indian settlements and the lifestyle and language of the people of New Mexico, but advises on food and travel, animals and packing, and hunting and camping. He brings the western adventure alive. A number of diarists listed here thought so highly of Gregg's prose that they incorporated it into their own diaries.

118. GRIFFIN, JOHN S.

A Doctor Comes to California: Griffin, Assistant Surgeon with Kearny's Dragoons, 1846–1847. San Francisco: California Historical Society, 1943. The Griffin journal is in the Bancroft Library.

Griffin provides a daily record of events as he moved along the Gila Trail under General Kearny's command. It is significant because it is one of only three first-hand accounts of the 1846 march of the Army of the West and supplements those by the other two reporters, William Emory (*114*) and Abraham Johnston (*120*). Griffin remained in California and later earned respect as one of the state's outstanding medical men.

119. HAGUE, HARLAN

"The First California Trail: The Southern Route." *Overland Journal* 5 (Winter 1987):41–50. *The Road to California: The Search for a Southern Overland Route, 1540–1848.* Glendale, Calif.: The Arthur H. Clark Company, 1978.

Harlan Hague's excellent studies trace the evolution of trails through the southwestern United States beginning with the Coronado expedition in 1540. Maps show the development of routes by Spanish explorers and padres, trappers, frontiersmen, emigrants, and military men. It is required reading for anyone interested in Southern Route history. A fine bibliography of both primary and secondary sources is included.

120. JOHNSTON, ABRAHAM ROBINSON

"Journal of Abraham Robinson Johnston, 1846," edited by Ralph P. Bieber. *Marching With the Army of the West, 1846–1848.* Vol. 4, Southwest Historical Series. Glendale, Calif.: The Arthur H. Clark Company, 1936.

Johnston was General Kearny's aide-de-camp and accompanied the 1846 expedition to California. His journal of the trip along the Gila Trail is detailed, full of description, and makes good reading. Johnston was killed at the Battle of San Pasqual a few days after his arrival in California.

121. LAMAR, HOWARD R.

Texas Crossings: The Lone Star State and the American Far West, 1836–1986. Austin: University of Texas Press, 1991.

Lamar discusses the numerous efforts made to establish overland trails through Texas and how those efforts were fueled by the gold rush to California in 1849. He provides a number of accurate maps and a fine bibliography.

122. LINDSAY, DIANA ELAINE

Our Historic Desert. San Diego, Calif.: Copley Press, Inc., 1973.

After crossing the Colorado River into California, the emigrants' trail went through what later became Anza Borrego Desert State Park. Lindsay writes about the sites and describes the terrain travelers crossed on the way to Warner's Ranch.

123. MARCY, RANDOLPH B.

The Prairie Traveler, A Handbook for Overland Expeditions. London: Trübner and Co., 1863.

Though not available to the forty-niner, this is an excellent source for the researcher. Marcy offers advice to the overlander and compiles a list of existing emigrant trails along with a record of routes, mileage, watering spots, and camping places.

124. MARTIN, MABELLE EPPARD

"California Emigrant Roads Through Texas," *Southwestern Historical Quarterly* 28 (1924 1925):287–301.

Gold discovery gave Texans an incentive to look at their vast state and explore the possibility of locating roads to Coons' Ranch and El Paso del Norte, where emigrants could funnel in to the Southern Trail. Martin provides a good description of the opening of the Upper or Emigrant Road and the Lower or Military Road, and relates some of the stories about the emigrants who took them.

125. MCARTHUR, PRISCILLA

Arkansas in the Gold Rush. Little Rock, Ark.: August House, 1986.

McArthur set out to assemble all the known records of the Arkansas goldseekers. These consist mainly of newspaper accounts, most of which were previously published by Grant Foreman *(116)* and/or Ralph Bieber *(100)*. She has located a small amount of new material, including an interesting diary by a woman who stayed at home. Appendices list Arkansas emigrating companies and reproduce the articles of association of several of them. Unfortunately, the map chosen to illustrate the route, by Donald Dale Jackson (1980), mistakes Apache Pass, Arizona, for Guadalupe Pass, New Mexico; neglects to route travelers through Santa Cruz, Sonora; and has argonauts negotiating the Algodones Dunes in California, instead of dipping into Mexico for that segment of the journey.

126. MÖLLHAUSEN, BALDWIN

Diary of a Journey From the Mississippi to the Coasts of the Pacific. London: Longman, Brown, Green, Longmans, & Roberts, 1858.

The colorful German scientist traveled with the Whipple railroad survey in 1853, sketched the topography, and created illustrations for the final report. This book contains splendid descriptions of the sights that emigrants traveling south of the Canadian River viewed and wrote about. Möllhausen eventually returned to Europe and wrote approximately fifty novels that earned him the title of the "German Fenimore Cooper."

127. OAKLEY, FRANCILE B.

"Arkansas' Golden Army of '49," *Arkansas Historical Quarterly* 6 (Spring 1947):1-79.

Oakley used the meager sources available to her in 1947 to recreate the history of gold rush trails out of Arkansas and the emigrants' adventures on the Fort Smith–Santa Fe Trail. There is little that is new here; she mainly paraphrases Grant Foreman's *(116)* work, which included material from eastern newspapers.

128. ORMSBY, WATERMAN L.

The Butterfield Overland Mail, edited by Lyle H. Wright and Josephine M. Bynum. San Marino, Calif.: The Huntington Library, 1942.

Ormsby enjoyed the distinction of being the only through passenger on the first westbound stage between Tipton, Missouri, and San Francisco, California, in 1858. The narrative consists of six articles that he wrote for the *New York Herald* describing his experience. This book is included because the route utilized portions of the lower Gila Trail, the

Apache Pass Trail, and the Upper Emigrant Road in Texas, and
Ormsby's observations could be of assistance in locating sites that forty-
niners described.

129. PETERSON, CHARLES S.

Mormon Battalion Trail Guide. Salt Lake City: Utah State
Historical Society, 1972.

Peterson has traced the march of the Mormon Battalion from Fort
Leavenworth to San Diego, California, from the diaries and journals of
those on the trip. He includes topographic maps on which he has marked
what he believes to be the route followed. Researchers should keep in
mind that much new information became available during the 1990s
resulting from on-site reconnaissance.

130. RUHLEN, GEORGE

"Kearny's Route from the Rio Grande to the Gila River,"
New Mexico Historical Review 32 (July 1957):213–230.

Using William Emory's *Notes* (*114*), Ruhlen commenced a careful
reconnaissance of the probable route that General Kearny and his troops
would have taken after leaving the Rio Grande near Truth or Consequences, New Mexico, in 1846. In addition to comparing landmarks
with old and recent maps, Ruhlen interviewed a number of pioneer
ranchers who knew the area well. He claims that he has correctly mapped
the route between the river and the Santa Rita mines. There was no ves-
tige of trail, but in concluding his article, Ruhlen wrote that his plotted
route meets all tests as the true route that Kearny followed. As far as we
know, no other researcher has gone into the field to try and uphold or
dispute the claim.

131. TYLER, DANIEL

*Concise History of the Mormon Battalion in the Mexican War,
1846–1847.* Salt Lake City: n.p., 1881.

Tyler was a volunteer in the Mormon Battalion, and his diary is probably the best to consult along with Philip St. George Cooke's report
(104) for background on the opening of a wagon road to the Pacific
Coast over the Southern Trail. There are many other reports and diaries
by members of the Mormon Battalion that should be studied for various
points of view. This is considered one of the better accounts.

132. UNITED STATES WAR DEPARTMENT

Reports of Explorations and Surveys, to Ascertain the Most Practicable and Economical Route For a Railroad From the Mississippi River to the Pacific Ocean. Washington, D.C.: A.O.P Nicholson, Printer, 1855–1860.

The twelve-volume set includes reports, maps, and sketches of the terrain along with botanical and zoological specimens. It is a valuable resource for learning about the southwestern landscape. Volume 7 is particularly pertinent to this study and includes a report of explorations from the Pima villages to the Rio Grande.

133. WARE, JOSEPH E.

The Emigrants' Guide to California. Reprinted from the 1849 edition with introduction and notes by John Caughey. Princeton, N.J.: Princeton University Press, 1932.

Ware published the first guidebook for California emigrants early in 1849. In addition to counseling the emigrant on health, food, routine, and equipment, the author outlined four routes for the traveler: over the plains and Sierra Nevada; by way of Panama; around the Horn; and across Mexico from Vera Cruz. It lists mileage for those who planned to take the Santa Fe or Southern trails.

134. WHIPPLE, AMIEL WEEKS

The Whipple Report, Journal of an Expedition from San Diego, California, to the Rio Colorado, from September 11 to December 11, 1849, edited and introduced by E. I. Edwards. Los Angeles: Westernlore Press, 1961. *Pathfinder in the Southwest: The Itinerary of Lieutenant A. W. Whipple During His Explorations For a Railway Route From Fort Smith to Los Angeles in the Years 1853 & 1854,* edited and annotated by Grant Foreman. Norman: University of Oklahoma Press, 1941.

Lieutenant Amiel W. Whipple was assigned to survey the United States-Mexico boundary. While camped near the Indian village of San Felipe, California, he wrote about the condition of emigrant parties as they rested from the rigors of their desert march. Whipple's short report mainly records weather conditions, mileage, and notes pertinent to his survey.

The second publication contains Whipple's 1854 map that traces the probable trail from Zuni to its termination at the junction of the Salt and Gila rivers southwest of Phoenix, Arizona. More detail is found in a map by Whipple and Lieutenant J. C. Ives: *Territory of New Mexico, Explorations and Surveys for a Rail Route from the Mississippi River to the Pacific Ocean*, Route Near the 35th Parallel from the Rio Grande to the Pacific Ocean. Washington, D.C.: Honorable Jefferson Davis, Secretary of War, 1853-1854.

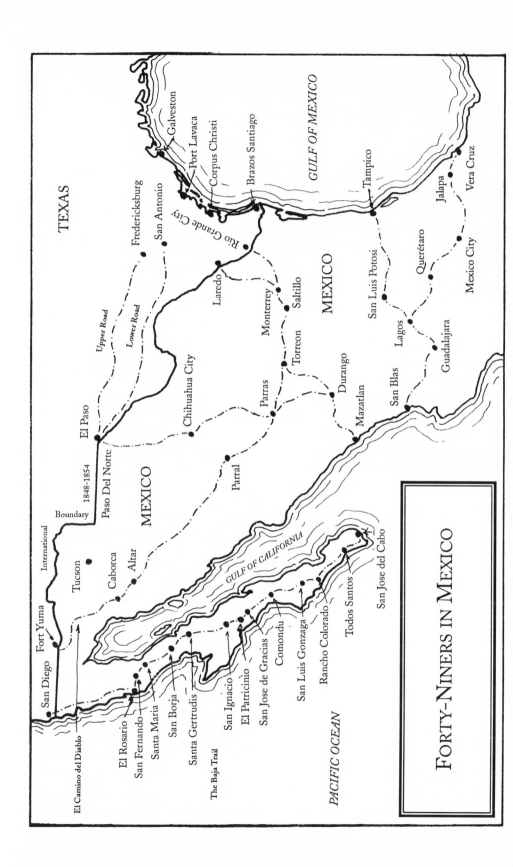

FORTY-NINERS IN MEXICO

FORTY-NINERS ON THE
MEXICAN GOLD TRAIL

INTRODUCTION

In the minority, but no less important, is the group of emigrants who decided to go to California by way of Mexico. I calculate that approximately 6,000 forty-niners crossed the country in 1849. This is a tough figure to substantiate because goldseekers arrived in Mexico at a number of points, and records were not kept as accurately as they are today. Travelers who briefly dipped into Mexico to join the Southern Trail at Guadalupe Pass, New Mexico, are listed with those who trod Southern Route trails.

The argonauts considered a number of widely advertised travel options. From collected diaries and letters, we learn that a number of them sailed out of East Coast ports or New Orleans and landed on Texas soil at Galveston, Port Lavaca, Corpus Christi, or Brazos Santiago. Once organized into wagon and/or pack trains, they moved west to the Rio Grande, crossed into Old Mexico, and headed for the seaport of Mazatlán by way of Monterrey, Saltillo, and Durango. A few companies followed Texas trails to Coons' Ranch and El Paso del Norte, turned south on the Chihuahua road to Durango, then went west to Mazatlán. Another popular choice was to sail to Vera Cruz, then take in the sights in Jalapa, Mexico City, and Guadalajara, before moving on to the seaports of San Blas or Mazatlán. Records show that a handful took ships to

Tampico, then eased along a tortuous mountain trail through San Luis Potosí and Lagos before getting to San Blas. They all expected to re-board ships on Mexico's Pacific coast and sail to San Francisco. But for many, it was not that easy.

Some spunky individuals abandoned rotting and leaky hulks on the Baja coast and trudged that peninsula's forbidding terrain to San Diego. Scholars have been silent on that aspect of the California trip, yet the account of the Baja experience is without parallel in the gold rush literature and adds new dimension to the overland adventure. There are eight records about that experience.

Why choose the Mexico crossing? The men believed they could travel faster—we know of no women who trod through Mexico—and they knew that if all went well, a traveler on the Mexican route could be in California in less than five months. Mexico's mild climate meant that visitors did not have to wait for snows to melt and the grass to appear. They also expected to find long-traveled roads, mainly through settled areas, where they could obtain food and lodging. Too, a number of goldseekers had served in Mexico during the recent war and were more or less familiar with the territory. Finally, there were those who chose the route simply for the adventure of it.

A number of travelers brought their ethnocentric biases along, while others were actually curious to learn about what was to them an exotic culture. Some, freed from Victorian restraints, took on the image of what later became known as the "ugly American" and made themselves unpopular with the natives. There were also a number of sophisticates, who not only could speak the Spanish language fluently but enjoyed a simpatico relationship with the Mexicans. While these adventurers tell their stories, we learn a good deal about the various routes along with an enormous amount of ethnographic and historic detail. Sadly, we also learn about devastation of roads and land, and poverty resulting from the Mexican War.

THE COURTYARD OF A MEXICAN HOTEL.
"We spread our blankets on the boards of the second floor, disturbing large colonies of fleas who held preemption rights . . . the whole night through, there was one continual braying and uproar from the two hundred hungry mules"—A/C/Ferris *148*:669.
Reproduction from the Arizona Historical Society Library,
The Century Illustrated Monthly Magazine 42 (September 1891.

Following are thirty-four stories, each one unique, all of them unforgettable, that recreate the Mexican experience in 1849. A number of reference works are listed for further study following the reminiscences. Some of the material listed here is in part adapted from my earlier publication in the *Bulletin of Bibliography (176).*

Well-preserved section of El Camino Real, Baja, California,
south of Santa Gerturdis and close to El Rosario.
Photograph courtesy Harry W. Crosby.

FORTY-NINERS ON THE
MEXICAN GOLD TRAIL

SOURCES

135. ANONYMOUS

"Account of a Journey to California via Texas and Mexico (Saltillo, Durango, Mazatlan) by Ship to San Francisco, Life in the Mines, and Return via Panama." Manuscript in the Huntington Library.

This nameless pioneer boarded the *Clara* on February 2 with the Mississippi Rangers and landed in Corpus Christi, Texas, on March 15. Though he wrote years after the fact and leaves out details, certain experiences remained stamped in his memory. For example, he tells how he and his comrades invested in 500 mules and hired Mexicans to drive them. As might be expected, the mule skinners and the gringos had communication difficulties, and some lives were lost as they attempted to settle the matter. After arriving in Mazatlán this argonaut booked passage on the *Grey Eagle* and arrived in San Francisco without further incident. He reminisced about his experiences in the northern mining district until February 1851, when he boarded the *Victoria* and sailed home via Panama. [TM-BT]

136. ANONYMOUS

Letter to parents from Guadalajara, May 3, 1849. Manuscript, AC#95A-09, in the Manuscript Society Information Exchange Database, University Libraries, Arizona State University, Tempe.

The writer, known only as Caspar, sailed from Vermont to Vera Cruz and made his way to Guadalajara by way of Mexico City. He describes some of the conditions in Mexico since the 1848 war, noting that the company had to travel in small groups since poverty was so acute that a group of fifty travelers was "enough to create a famine in a Mexican Village . . ." This group was typical of many—it learned that passage to San Francisco could be as much as $125 without provisions. Since funds were running short, an option was to cover the thousand-plus miles to San Diego on foot, which would include a trek over the forbidding El Camino del Diablo. [MX-]

137. BAKER, GEORGE HOLBROOK, 1827–1906

"Records of a California Journey," *Quarterly, Society of California Pioneers* 7 (1930):217–243.

Baker caught the "prevailing infection" on hearing about California's bonanza, dropped his studies at New York's Academy of Design, and headed west with a group of high-spirited young men, the New England Pioneers (p. 219). They sailed to Vera Cruz on the *Nancy Bishop*, then set their sights for Mexico City on the National Road, which was in rough shape since both American and Mexican armies had done their best to destroy it during the Mexican War. Baker ultimately arrived in Mazatlán, where friends persuaded him to help finance purchase of the schooner *Diana*, boasting they could run her up the coast in twenty-five days. Eighteen days and 300 miles later, the vessel began taking on water. Fearing that one good storm would finish her, Baker abandoned ship at San Jose del Cabo. Since his investment had left him with sixty-two cents, he was challenged to raise funds by playing physician and curing sickness among the natives. This endeavor soon earned him enough to purchase passage on the schooner *Josephine*.

Baker went to the mines for a time, but settled down in 1855 to edit and publish Sacramento's *Spirit of the Age*. Next, he took on the city's first evening newspaper, the *Granite Journal*, which expired in 1856 (Kemble 1962:213, 269, 323). During this time, he produced a number of lithographic sketches said to be among the most authentic pictures of California during the early days of the gold rush. He eventually moved to San Francisco, where he became an independent lithographer (Peters 1935:47–54). [MX-BT]

138. BLAKE, CHARLES MORRIS, 1819–1893

"Dr. Charles Morris Blake," *Pacific Medical Journal* 36 (1893):577–579.

Blake traveled with Edwin Sherman (*165*) and Daniel Woods (*169*) as far as San Blas, where he boarded the thirty-five- ton schooner *San Blasena*. J. D. B. Stillman consulted Blake's journal and read that Blake resolved to abandon the vessel if he "was ever permitted to reach land again" (*181* 1875:244). Edwin Sherman confirmed that Blake did indeed abandon ship when it put in to San Jose del Cabo on May 19, 1849 (*165*:279). The hike to San Diego was tortuous, and Stillman copied the following from Blake's diary: "but such a route over fields of burning sand, across elevated plateaus of ancient lava, pumice, obsidian, and trap-dikes, encompassed by thorny rigid shrubs that never had a name—looking with hope and apprehension in every ravine for water and rattlesnakes . . ." (*181* 1875:246). The location of the original journal is not known.

Blake later founded St. Augustine College for boys in Benicia, California; taught and preached in South America; served on Major General Frémont's staff during the Civil War; commanded a company of black soldiers at Morris Island; and spent time in Arizona Territory. Then he enrolled in the University of California, where he earned a medical degree in 1876. [MX-BJ]

139. BONESTELL, LOUIS HENRY, 1827-1919

"Autobiography," *Quarterly, Society of California Pioneers* 4 (1927):117-135.

Bonestell "decided to be in the lead" and get to California before the gold ran out. He joined a group of men—200 in all—who each put up seven dollars (plus provisions), chartered the bark *Mara*, then set sail for Vera Cruz. The men trekked across Mexico to San Blas, where they boarded the *Dolphin*, high on hope they would be in San Francisco before thirty days had passed. Thirty days soon passed and the *Dolphin* was only approaching Santo Domingo, about half way up the Baja coast. Reasoning that it would be far safer to walk, Bonestell and forty-three companions went ashore on May 26, 1849, and resolutely set out for San Diego. Each carried a claret bottle of water, half a pound of rice, two pieces of hardtack, a couple of blankets, and some cooking utensils. The wanderers soon learned to savor the taste of horse and rattlesnake meat, lizards, birds, and any other game they could find. All the time they thirsted for water. Three men whose reminiscences are included here— John Clark (*140*), Samuel Crane (*141*), and John Griffith (*149*)—were members of this group.

Bonestell and friends had no idea where they were, but after a few days of wandering, came on the mission trail by chance and reached San Fernando on June 4. The men arrived in San Diego on June 22, 1849, ragged, penniless, and hungry, but grateful to be alive. Bonestell remained in San Diego for awhile, and one August day, while he was looking out to sea, a strange ship without rigging and sails drifted to port. It was the *Dolphin*. He watched while her passengers came safely to shore. Then the old tub was condemned and sunk.

From his autobiography, we learn that Bonestell continued his trade of carpentry and published a short-lived newspaper in San Francisco, *Wide West*. He ultimately founded a merchandising business in San Francisco and Oakland, which he ran until his death. [MX-BJ]

140. CLARK, JOHN R.

"The Schooner Dolphin—A Perilous Voyage," by J. R. C. *Newark (N.J.) Daily Advertiser,* September 14, 1849.

Clark wrote that he was among the passengers on the *Dolphin* when it sailed out of Mazatlán on April 23, 1849, noting that its captain, A. R. Winslow, was not "fit to command an oyster boat and did not take water enough on board to last us more than 20 or 25 days . . ." Clark abandoned ship on the Baja coast with Samuel Crane (*141*), Louis Bonestell (*139*), and John Griffith (*149*), whose stories appear here. The J. R. C. of this letter was identified by Samuel Crane. [MX-BJ]

141. CRANE, SAMUEL P.

"Diary of a Journey to California—Privations, &c," *Newark (N.J.) Daily Advertiser,* September 26, 1849.

Crane was another who gratefully left the *Dolphin*, and his story supplements those of Bonestell (*139*), Clark (*140*), and Griffith (*149*). He said that he arrived in San Diego in a "truly California suit . . . As to boots and shoes, I was the fortunate possessor of one of each . . . my pantaloons excelled Joseph's coat in variety of hues . . . being patched and stayed with pieces of old shirt, blanket, old soldier's clothes. I had but one shirt, a flannel one, minus a sleeve, nearly half a hat, sundry parts of the brim and crown having parted company on different occasions in the immediate vicinity of a cactus prickly pear. As to coat, I had none, and altogether cut a woeful figure."

J. D. B. Stillman wrote in *Seeking the Golden Fleece* (*181* 1877:331) that Crane later wrote about his experience on the peninsula. That document has not been located. [MX-BJ]

142. DODGE, HENRY LEE, 1825–1902

"Statement and Biographical Sketch." Manuscript (ca. 1888) in the Bancroft Library.

Dodge's reminiscences are mainly biographical, and he glosses over what was probably an uneventful trip to California. He notes, however, that he crossed to San Blas by way of Vera Cruz and Mexico City, and arrived in San Francisco in June, three and a half months after his departure from Montpelier, Vermont.

In subsequent years he founded a mercantile business in San Francisco, Dodge, Sweeney and Company; was superintendent of the San Francisco Mint; served on the Board of Supervisors and in the State Senate; and became a trustee of Stanford University (Eldredge 1915:412). [MX-BT]

143. DONAHUE, JAMES, 1824–1862

"Biographical Sketch." Manuscript (1886) in the Bancroft Library.

Donahue supervised the U.S. government foundry and machine shop at Brazos Santiago during the Mexican War. On learning about the gold discovery, he decided to cross Mexico on horseback and find passage to San Francisco, where he arrived without incident in the spring of 1849. He later formed the Union Iron Works with his brothers, Michael and Peter. The Donahues also established the San Francisco Gas Company; Joseph Green Eastland, whose story appears here (*145*), was the company's secretary for twenty-three years. [-BT]

144. DUNPHY, WILLIAM, 1829–1892

"Statement from William Dunphy." Manuscript (ca.1891) in the Bancroft Library.

Dunphy ran away from his home in Ireland when he was twelve, and ultimately ended up in Texas, where he joined John Hays's Texas Rangers (Milliken 1965:102). He set up a cattle business near Brownsville after the Mexican War, but on hearing news of gold discovery set out for Durango with forty companions. Dunphy and his friends managed more adventure than most during their brief sojourn in Mexico. As a matter of fact, this bunch of daredevils was fortunate to get out of the country alive. Dunphy wrote that the governor of Durango persuaded them to head for the mountains, where they spent fifteen days battling 500 Apaches. Presumably the freelancers earned a tidy sum for their efforts, but before it was over the men had buried one comrade and slowed pace to tend to the wounds of nine others.

Dunphy and company were one example of American travelers in Mexico who set aside restraints and showed little respect for the natives. The battle with the Apaches apparently did not alter their behavior. Once in Mazatlán the madcaps were astir again and randomly fired their pistols, causing residents to think the Americans had attacked once more. This Irishman must have had a protective angel, for he arrived in California unscathed and went straight to the mines near Tuolumne. A short time later, he settled down and opened a general store in Jamestown.

Ultimately, Dunphy became one of the largest stock and cattle dealers in the West with ranches throughout California and Nevada. *The San Francisco Call* wrote that the Irish orphan left an estate close to $6 million when he died (9/22/1892). [TM-BT]

145. EASTLAND, JOSEPH GREEN, 1831–1894

"Dictation." Manuscript (1886) in the Bancroft Library.

Joseph Eastland was eighteen when he started for California with his father, Thomas. These reminiscences add little new information to his father's more complete diary and letters (*146*).

The junior Eastland was among those who established the city of Mill Valley, California. He also founded the Oakland and Stockton gas companies. He was twice elected president of the Society of California Pioneers and served as president of St. Luke's Hospital, in addition to performing other good works. [TM-BT]

146. EASTLAND, THOMAS B., 1805–1864

"To California Through Texas and Mexico. The Diary and Letters of Thomas B. Eastland and Joseph G. Eastland, His Son." Foreword by Douglas S. Watson. Notes by Dorothy H. Huggins. *California Historical Society Quarterly* 17 (1939):99–133; 229–250.

Eastland and his son left Nashville, Tennessee, on April 21, 1849, for New Orleans, where they boarded the steamship *Fanny*. After landing in Port Lavaca, Texas, the two made their way to San Antonio, where Texas Ranger John Coffee Hays was preparing to locate and mark out a wagon road to Coons' Ranch and El Paso del Norte. Thinking it would be good to have army protection, the Eastlands tagged along. They ultimately regretted that decision since it took ninety-seven days to cover the 693 miles to Coons' Ranch, where they arrived on September 11. Fortunately, Eastland wrote a comprehensive diary, thus leaving a rare account of travel on what he called a "shameful route," but one that would quickly become a major thoroughfare—Texas's Lower or Military Road.

Leaving the troops, the Eastlands turned south to the city of Chihuahua, then continued over a difficult and dangerous trail that wound over the Sierra Madre Occidental. On arrival in Mazatlán, the Eastlands paid for passage on the steamer *Oregon* and arrived in San Francisco without incident on December 1, 1849.

The senior Eastland acquired a number of mining claims and invested in town lots for resale in the new town of Oro, on the Bear River. He returned to Tennessee in 1853, stopping off in Washington, D.C., where he tried unsuccessfully to obtain an appointment as surveyor of the Port of San Francisco. Eastland returned to California in 1864, just a few months before his death. [TM-BT]

147. EMERSON, WILLIAM HENRY, 1830–1897

"A Memoranda of the principle [*sic*] incidents, time of my departure from home, dates of my arrival and the principle ranches and towns on the way, also the names and ages of the company." Manuscript (1849) in the California State Library, Sacramento.

Emerson began his diary on February 25, 1849, writing the final entry on July 20, 1849, when he arrived in San Francisco. He started out from Richmond, Virginia, and made his way to Cincinnati and New Orleans, where he sailed to Brownsville, Texas. He headed for "Musatland" [Mazatlán] by way of Monterrey, Parras, and Durango, carefully recording and describing the towns and places he passed along the way. Emerson included some nice sketches.

At the time of his death, Emerson was employed as a bottler at Bartlett Springs and died of blood poisoning after a glass cut, according to the *San Francisco Call* on June 19, 1897. [MX-BT]

148. FERRIS, A. C.

"To California in 1849 through Mexico," *The Century Illustrated Monthly Magazine* 42 (May–October 1891):666-679.

Ferris and the 200-man Manhattan-Overland Association set sail on the chartered bark *Mara*. They landed at Vera Cruz February 24, then moved westward along General Winfield Scott's route through Mexico City, Guadalajara, and San Blas. He remembers the Cerro Gordo battlefield, "where Santa Anna made his most stubborn fight," describing the "scattered uncoffined bones, and ghastly skulls...[that] gave silent witness of the awful struggles of our little army" (p. 673). The wounds were still fresh, and antipathy toward Americans was strong, so Ferris and his army of red-shirted and well-armed horsemen faced hostility wherever they went. Crowds tried to dismount them in Jalapa; folks in Mexico City pushed them to their knees and removed their hats during a religious procession; and on seeing the forty-niners enter Guadalajara, soldiers raised their arms and citizens scattered, shouting, "Revolution!" In spite of these travails, the group made it safely to San Blas, where they found passage on the *Cayuga*, arriving at the Golden Gate on May 14. Ferris claimed that his was the first organized group to reach that port by sea and by land. His prose is enlivened by Frederic Remington illustrations.

He returned to Hackensack, New Jersey, in December and recounted his "Hardships of the Isthmus in '49," in *The Century Illustrated* 19 (1890–1891):929–931. He also wrote extensively for the *San Jose (Calif.) Pioneer*, which published the story of his sojourn in California in a twelve-part series beginning February 24, 1883. [MX-BT]

149. GRIFFITH, JOHN W.

"Cruise of the Dolphin," in *Seeking the Golden Fleece*, J. D. B. Stillman. San Francisco, 1877. Pp. 331–359. Microfiche. Louisville, Ky. Lost Cause Press, 19–. "The Lost Argonauts: The Journal of John W. Griffith." Carbon typescript (1876) in the Bancroft Library.

Griffith landed in Vera Cruz off the *Mara*. He was among sixty-eight impatient goldseekers who crowded into the rotting hulk *Dolphin* at Mazatlán. At the end of twenty-five days, with food and water supplies depleted, Griffith left the boat near Punto Santo Domingo on the Baja coast and hoofed it to San Diego with Louis Bonestell (*139*), John Clark (*140*), and Samuel Crane (*141*). He tells of slow progress toward San Fernando over a terrain of sharp, loose rocks and how he suffered from lack of water, resorting to the fruit of the prickly pear in spite of its lacerating thorns. More often than not, the men did not even know where they were. They were desperate by the time they reached the San Fernando Mission on June 4, where Griffith admitted to compelling a poor resident to harvest his unripe wheat and make it into mush. Like his friends, he was happy at last to get to San Diego.

Griffith later worked for the Miles brothers, who ran a mill, warehouse, commission, and ranching enterprise in Los Angeles County (*178*:34; Thompson 1880:185). [MX-BT]

150. GUNN, LEWIS CARSTAIRS, 1813–1892

Records of a California Family, edited by Anna Lee Marston. San Diego, Calif.: n.p.,1928.

Lewis Gunn left Philadelphia for New Orleans on March 10, 1849, where he planned to embark for Brazos Santiago on the steamer *Globe.* He carried a little leather journal in which he faithfully penned the details of each day's events, thus leaving an accurate record of sights and scenes along the way. The doctor and his party crossed the Rio Grande to Matamoros on the first leg of a trip that would take them to Monterrey, Parras, Durango, and Mazatlán. But first, they had to reduce 2,600 pounds of luggage to manageable proportions for the four mules.

They finally made it to Durango on June 7. Like many who were curious about Mexican customs, Gunn attended a bullfight, where he saw "old Spain all over again, only without the spirit and daring courage." And like all other Americans, he took sides with the bull. The trip to Mazatlán took seventy-eight days. After the usual hassle in finding passage, he embarked on the *Copiano.* Compared to the majority who told of wretched voyages, Gunn had a relatively serene trip to California.

Part 2 of the book recreates life in the bustling, cosmopolitan mining town of Sonora, where Gunn practiced medicine and published the *Sonora (Calif.) Herald.* Parts 3 and 4 were written by his wife, Elizabeth, and contain reminiscences of her trip around the Horn and life in Sonora and San Francisco. [MX-BT]

151. HARDIN, ROBERT S., 1822–1899

"Diary." Manuscript (1849) in the Department of Special Collections, Manuscripts Division, Stanford University Libraries.

Researchers who want to know what a traveler might have had to lay out to go from Springfield, Kentucky, to San Francisco by way of Mexico will find the exact figures here since Hardin accounted for every penny. He thought that $105 would cover his expenses; alas, he spent $611.18 by the time the Peruvian bark *Fanny*, docked at the Golden Gate on May 25, 1849. Hardin started out on the Mexican leg of his journey from Mier on March 4 and headed for Mazatlán by way of Durango. He had a fairly easy crossing, though he complained about sore feet and the constant attack by fleas that flourished in the Mexican *mésons*. Hardin spent his time on the *Fanny* recording the daily latitude, longitude, and weather conditions. He wrote about his first few weeks in mines not far from Sacramento, again carefully recording every expense. A number of forty-niners traveled with their slaves, and Hardin brought his servant Abe along. He appears to have been tolerant of the fact that Abe enjoyed downing strong spirits now and then. However, Abe got the short end of the stick on July 1, 1849, when he panned dust worth $13.20; Hardin noted his own portion would be $12.80. The last entry was on December 24, 1849, when he wrote: "Spent the day very unpleasantly, and disagreeably—could not enjoy the Sabbath—thought of Home."

Hardin soon tired of mining and commenced farming in the Sacramento Valley. After a time, he moved to Pope Valley, Napa County, where he spent the rest of his life, according to a note appended to the manuscript. [MX-BT]

152. HAWKS, JAMES D.

"A Forty-Niner in Baja California," edited by Walt Wheelock. *Brand Book II.* San Diego, Calif.: The Westerners, 1971. "The Diary of James D. Hawks," *Quarterly, Society of California Pioneers* 6 (1929):83–96. The manuscript copy is held in the Society archives and includes sketches of mission churches and ranchos. "Journal of the Expedition of Mr. J. D. Hawks and Party, Through the Interior of the Peninsula of Lower California from San Domingo to San Diego," in *Resources of the Pacific Slope*, by J. Ross Browne. New York: D. Appleton and Company, 1869.

Hawks sailed for Panama on the steamer *Falcon*, which left New York in March 1849. It is apparent that his original intention was to cross the Isthmus and continue by sea to San Francisco, for he did sail out of Panama on the schooner *San Juan* on April 21. The ship put in at Santo

Domingo, on the Pacific coast of Baja, California, on August 10, after 111 days at sea. Hawks does not write why he and five companions left the schooner, but we can guess that they were dissatisfied with the ship's progress. In spite of adverse circumstances, he managed to keep a very interesting record of progress over the desolate Baja terrain, which included stops at Ramón Aguilar's Rancho El Patrocino, San Ignacio, Rancho San Martin, Santa Gertrudis, and Mission San Borja. The diarist met other Americans along the trail, among them a group who had been left stranded by the schooner *Jose Cascaras*. "I can scarcely imagine that there is a worse country than this to travel through, with nothing to subsist on except the fruit of the cactus and the few figs which we find at the missions," Hawks wrote on September 1 as he plodded toward San Diego. [BT-BJ]

153. HOOPER, H. O.

"To California in '49," *Overland Monthly* 22 (1893): 318–329.

Hooper's ten-month saga was filled with misadventure, but he said that his prior experience at sea and in a cavalry regiment during the Mexican War served him well. He left St. Louis on December 28, 1848, and headed for Fredericksburg, Texas, where he teamed up with sixty other greenhorns. This appears to be one of the earliest groups to set out for El Paso del Norte, because Hooper indicates the road was unmarked: "the sun was our only guide . . ." (p. 320). One day, while he and two friends were trailing the pack, the Comanches attacked. Hooper managed to conceal himself, but his companions were not so lucky and were killed and scalped. So Hooper wandered on alone until by chance, a Mexican family rescued, fed, and clothed him, then provided a horse and guide for the rest of his trip to El Paso del Norte. His fortunes changed for awhile, and he reached Mazatlán safely, but his ship *Roland* ran aground in a violent storm, smashed to pieces, and sank with twenty-two still on board. Hooper washed ashore without a scratch. (George McKnight was another who survived the wreck, *157*.) Hooper pulled himself together one more time, hired on as a sailor on the *Dos Amigos* and reached San Francisco in October. [TM-BT]

154. JORDAN, RUDOLPH, 1818–1910

"An Autobiography," *Quarterly, Society of California Pioneers* 4 (December 1927):174–201.

Wanderlust hit Jordan when he was twenty-six, and he set out for Havana, where he found work producing daguerreotypes. When he heard the golden news, he quickly settled his accounts, boarded the *Luchana*, and disembarked at Vera Cruz on December 1, 1848. Jordon hired a stage to take him to Jalapa, where he purchased horses and hired a guide for the cross-country ride. During this time, he demonstrated his understanding of Mexican feelings toward Americans, and resolved to take no part in any possible clash by avoiding the use of the English language. He managed to stay out of trouble for the first part of his journey. But his temper flared in San Blas, where he exchanged blows and a few rocks with a sea captain who refused to set sail or reimburse prepaid passage. Jordan eventually received satisfaction but prudently rode north to Mazatlán, where he boarded the Peruvian bark *Fanny*.

He landed in San Francisco on May 25 and headed for Sonora, where he made a big strike at Jackass Gulch. He used the money to start up a successful mining supply business. He also dabbled in real estate and at one time developed a vineyard and olive orchard in Napa County. This interesting man also turned down Alfred B. Nobel's proposition to market his new product, nitroglycerin, for use in the mines; Jordan felt it was much too dangerous in its present form. [MX-BT]

155. KNAPP, W. AUGUSTUS

"An Old Californian's Pioneer Story," *Overland Monthly* 10 (October 1887):389–408.

Knapp wrote that he was engaged as secretary to an expedition led by Colonel Sam Whiting, formerly of Texas (not to be confused with Lieutenant W. H. C. Whiting, who led a team to survey a viable route between San Antonio and Coons' Ranch). The trip was a disaster. Whiting had no knowledge of the road, and disregarding advice to limit supplies to 1,500 pounds, loaded up with five tons of *panoche* (ground parched corn and sugar), bacon, and other provisions in equal proportion. Because there was sparse feed on the dry Texas plains and even less water, the animals soon gave out, and the emigrants were forced to leave supplies and wagons behind. Nevertheless, they plodded on, now in footgear of rawhide. They finally reached El Paso—six months after starting out.

Knapp was ill by the time they reached town. By chance, Sara Bowman, better known as the Great Western, took him in and nursed him until he was well enough to travel. Knapp ultimately started for Mazatlán via Durango. At one point he lost the trail and was ambushed and wounded by Mescalero Apaches. The Indians took him to their camp, where they kept him suspended in a hammock about eight feet above the ground. The chief's daughter took charge, and Knapp wrote that she "cared for me kindly enough in the way of binding up my wounds with soothing remedies; and when I was able to eat she gave me parched corn and a sort of mush made from grass seed with square chunks of buffalo meat" (p. 397). Choosing a moment when the Indians were otherwise occupied, Knapp stole an Apache mount and escaped. He made it to Mazatlán, where he climbed aboard the *Abeille* and arrived in San Francisco on December 27, 1849. [TM-BT]

156. McGAFFEY, JOSEPH WYATT, 1824–1849

"Across Mexico in the Days of '49," *Touring Topics* 24 (May 1929):18–49.

Joseph McGaffey graduated from Dartmouth College, where he had been a classmate of Daniel Webster. The relationship appears to be one reason he decided to go to Corpus Christi and join a group called Kinney's Rangers, a venture promoted by Henry Lawrence Kinney, formerly a suitor of Daniel Webster's daughter. Kinney advertised the route through Mexico, hoping to attract emigrants to his area. McGaffey left Boston on February 24, 1849, on the schooner *I. W. Herbert Lewis* and sailed into Corpus Christi a month later. McGaffey barely discusses details of the trip across Mexico since cholera raged through his camp and eight comrades succumbed to the disease within days. He made the following comment in his diary: "O thou messenger of Death, when will thy hand be stayed?" Ultimately the survivors made it to Mazatlán and found passage to California (p. 49). The trials of the trip wore down his health, and McGaffey died soon after his arrival in California. [TM-BT]

157. McKNIGHT, GEORGE, 1819–?

California 49er . . . Travels from Perrysburg to California. Perrysburg, Ohio: Andrews Printing Company, 1903. Pamphlet in the Bancroft Library. Also included is an August 21, 1849, letter to his brother John H. McKnight, which was published in the *Perrysburg (Ohio) Reveille*. The pamphlet is on microfilm: Western Americana, Reel 349, no. 3420. New Haven, Conn.: Research Publications.

McKnight joined up with George W. B. Evans (*46*) and the Defiance (Ohio) Gold Hunters' Expedition. These forty-niners went to Eagle Pass on the Rio Grande and hired a guide to lead them west over Mexico's barren uplands, Serranías del Burro, before turning north to join the Southern Trail at Guadalupe Pass. George McKnight left the group at Chihuahua and crossed Mexico to Mazatlán by way of Durango. He survived the shipwreck of the *Roland* with H. O. Hooper (*153*). He wrote that he lost everything that night except what he was wearing, his watch, and $30. The twenty-seven-page pamphlet repeats a number of vignettes (or tall tales) of California happenings.

On October 27, 1934, the *Oakland Tribune* noted that George McKnight was known as the hero of Grass Valley. He stubbed his toe one day in 1850, looked down and found it was a hill of gold, and thus became responsible for the development of deep-rock mining in California. [MX-BT]

158. McNEIL, SAMUEL

McNeil's Travels in 1849, to, through and from the Gold Regions, in California. Columbus, Ohio: Scott and Bascomb Printers, 1850. Reprinted by Ye Galleon Press, Fairfield, Wash., 1989.

"Being a shoemaker, and ambitious to rise somewhat over the bench, it is no wonder that the discovery of gold in California excited my fancy and hopes . . ." and believing that "providence was influencing us to seek the gold regions," Samuel McNeil joined up with a group of men from Lancaster, Ohio, for the California journey (p. 2). This colorful character steamed out of New Orleans on the *Globe*, arriving in Brazos Santiago March 4. One of McNeil's companions was William Perkins, company captain, who also left a journal of the trip (*162*). McNeil had low regard of Perkins, saying that he was "an overbearing ignorant Englishman, who did not suit my republican principles" (p. 6). On the other hand, we wonder what Perkins might have thought about McNeil, who thought he was quite an impressive sight in Durango: "my beard reached almost to my knees, and consequently, with my long silver mounted rifle and other accoutrements, I presented a truly formidable appearance, and attracted general attention and admiration wherever I went" (p. 11).

McNeil arrived in San Francisco June 9 on the Danish schooner *Joanna & Oluffa*. He tried his luck in the northern mining district before opening a tent store in Sacramento. After making a modest sum he returned to Cincinnati on October 12, 1849. [MX-BT]

159. NYE, WILLIAM FOSTER, 1824–?

"Letter from San Francisco, July 6, 1849," *Newark (N.J.) Daily Advertiser,* September 17, 1849.

Nye quit the crowded bark *Mary Frances* at San Jose del Cabo and hiked the Baja terrain with W. C. S. Smith. Smith called him "a generous and self-denying friend, but an inveterate enemy; brave as a lion, yet gentle as a woman. Dear Nye! How can I do you justice?" (*166* 1995:129). The men had been told they would find "fine country" for the walk to San Diego. Instead, Nye found "a perfect desert; our path lay over barren plains of sand, or mountains of bare rocks." They had been lucky to start off with horses, but both animals and men suffered from lack of food and water. Ultimately, the animals gave out and Nye reported that they "were compelled to hoof it, shod with rawhide sandals." It took sixty days to reach San Diego, where they had their first full meal in some time—salt pork and hard bread—which seemed like "most luxurious fare." Nye completed his report with some observations on life in the diggings.

Nye, a Harvard Law School graduate, went to work in San Francisco building brick houses. He had had enough of California by 1855, when he went home to Sandwich, Massachusetts (Swift 1951). [MX-BJ]

160. PATTERSON, GEORGE WASHINGTON, 1822–1895

George Washington Patterson and the Founding of Ardenwood, by Keith E. Kennedy. Cupertino, Calif.: California History Center & Foundation, 1995. Patterson's holograph "Overland Journey, 1849, from Indiana to California" (1872), is in the Bancroft Library.

George Patterson was born in East Berlin, Pennsylvania, the son of Lydia and Henry Patterson (HAL 1883:957; Guinn 1904:982). He was residing in Indiana at the time of gold discovery and got together with twenty young men from Fayetteville who organized a joint-stock company, each contributing $500 toward expenses and supplies for the trip. In a letter to Hubert Howe Bancroft, Patterson said that "every man with blood in his veins and a few dollars in his pockets, or credit to borrow, turned head toward California—his heart was already there." The men sailed out of New Orleans to Port Lavaca, Texas, where they outfitted for a wagon trip and moved on to San Antonio. Wagon travel evidently did not set too well, so they traded accoutrements for pack horses before starting for Durango. Like others on Texas trails, the men suffered from lack of water and shortage of supplies. Patterson reached Durango in June, where he made his last entry, recording the cholera death of a comrade. At this point, he told Bancroft he did not have time to finish his story, and perhaps he (Bancroft) would not be interested anyway. We learn that he made it safely to Mazatlán, where he boarded the brig *Louisa* for San Francisco.

After mining on the American River for a time, he moved to Alameda County, where he purchased a farm and built his home, Ardenwood, which included a "fine deer park." Patterson was known to be an ardent supporter of public schools in the county (*San Francisco Call*, 9/13/1895). [TM-BT]

161. PATTERSON, LAWSON, B.

Twelve Years in the Mines of California; Embracing a General View of the Gold Region With Practical Observations on Hill, Placer, and Quartz Diggings; and Notes on the Origin of Gold Deposits. Cambridge, Mass.: Miles and Dillingham, 1862.

Patterson was generous toward the shipping lines, writing that they "were not very abundant, nor was steam communication in a very forward or flattering state. They who went forward in the early days, went expecting to rough it, and they were not disappointed in their expectations" (p. 35). This traveler left Boston on the *Col. Fanning*, arrived in Brazos Santiago on February 26, then packed to Mazatlán by way of Monterrey. He had expected to sail on the *Dolphin*, but one look was enough for him, and he climbed aboard the *Paridisto* instead. He arrived in San Francisco on July 20.

Patterson became a full-time miner and stayed in the business near Georgetown in Eldorado County for twelve years. His book should interest students of California mining history, as he wrote extensively about the miners, the towns, and his own experiences. [MX-BT]

162. PERKINS, WILLIAM, 1827–1893

Three Years in California. William Perkins' Journal of Life at

Sonora, 1849–1852, edited by Dale L. Morgan and James R. Scobil. Berkeley: University of California Press, 1964. Holograph manuscript, "El Campo de los Sonoraenses or Three Years Residence in California," by William Perkins (1849–1851), is in the Bancroft Library.

Perkins boarded the steamer *Globe* in New Orleans for the trip to Brazos Santiago. He wasted little time on arrival, and once organized and outfitted, headed for Mazatlán by way of Monterrey, Saltillo, and Durango. Perkins determined that the men under his leadership would follow custom, and saw to it that they removed their hats and guns during Good Friday observance in Monterrey. "The natives were taken by surprise," he wrote, "and pleased with our simple act of devotion and consideration for their religious feelings, were quite desarmed of their anger, and even cheered us heartily as we marched on..." (1964:78). In addition, General Jose Urrea, governor of Durango, treated Perkins to a nineteen-course dinner on his arrival in that city.

Thus these travelers went on to Mazatlán without incident. They sailed north on the *Joanna & Oluffa.* Perkins settled for awhile in Sonora, Tuolumne County, and ultimately wrote one of the best accounts of activities in that famous mining camp. Some time later, he moved to Rosario, Argentina, where he remained active in business and political affairs until his death. His manuscript is divided into forty-four chapters; the overland trip is recorded in chapter 1. [MX-BT]

163. PERRY, J. A.

Travels, Scenes and Sufferings, in Cuba, Mexico, California. Illustrated with engravings by Elder J. A. Perry. Boston: Redding & Co., 1853. The book and microfilm are in the Bancroft Library.

Perry left New York on February 3, 1849, aboard the *Columbus,* landed in Vera Cruz, and moved on to San Blas by way of Mexico City. This writer was an inveterate sightseer and penned lengthy descriptions of the natives, their towns, manners, and customs, though with a strong anti-Catholic bias. Nevertheless, there is much of interest in his vivid and detailed accounts of the churches, jails, bullfights, an execution, and a visit to a Mexico City torture chamber. Perry was one who refused to remove his hat near a cathedral and was repaid by the residents with a stone pelting.

He embarked on the *Edith* out of San Blas, saying that he was happy to leave the "thievish Mexicans" their "bigotry, superstition, priestcraft, and degradation, hoping the Americans will pity them and take the country and civilize and moralize the people." Perry sojourned about two years in California, then returned to Providence, Rhode Island, by way of Panama. [MX-BT]

164. SAYRE, THOMAS

"Diary of a Gold Seeker who Crossed Mexico from Tampico to Mazatlán in 1849." Manuscript (1849–1850) in the Bancroft Library.

Sayre was among those who landed in Tampico and crossed to San Blas via San Luis Potosí and Guadalajara, arriving on March 22, 1849. He was an observant traveler and provided a good deal of detail on the trip, made more interesting because of his colorful prose and creative spelling. Sayre was a fellow traveler in Daniel Woods's Camargo Company (*169*).

He sailed to San Francisco on the *Fanny*, writing that the passengers enlivened weary days on board by trying to catch dolphins. He arrived in California on May 25 and went to work at mines near Jacksonville. [MX-BT]

165. SHERMAN, EDWIN ALLEN, 1829–1914

"Sherman Was There: The Recollections of Major Edwin A. Sherman," introduced by Allen B. Sherman. *California Historical Society Quarterly* (1944):259–281, 349–377; (1945): 47–72, 165–180, 271–279. The Edwin Allen Sherman Papers (1872–1971) are in the Bancroft Library.

Sherman's "Personal Reminiscences of a California Pioneer of 1849" (Box 4, Folder 1), form the basis for the published version. Here is a mature and knowledgeable individual who details the trip between Tampico and Mazatlán and his subsequent life in California. This man had served with Generals William J. Worth, Zachary Taylor, and Winfield Scott during the Mexican War. With news of gold discovery, he assisted in organizing the Camargo Company, whose members Thomas Sayre (*164*) and Daniel Woods (*169*) are listed here. Charles M. Blake (*138*) traveled with them as far as Mazatlán. The company gathered in

Philadelphia and sailed to Tampico on February 1, 1849. Sherman put the war aside on his return to Mexico and paid his respects to men who were formerly his prisoners. As a result, he was enormously well treated on his journey across that country.

Sherman tells us he sailed on the *Fanny*, which was no different than other ships that season—overcrowded and undersupplied. He noted that the sweet potatoes "shrank in size and flavor, fresh pork ceased to squeal, and mutton to bleat, and the cattle moaned less, while the wails of the hungry passengers increased tenfold" (1944:275).

Sherman established a successful mining claim at Rose's Bar on the Yuba River until ill health compelled him to seek employment in Sacramento clerking for the transportation firm of Francis and Stewart. Over the years, he published numerous works on the Mexican War, Freemasonry, and other subjects. [MX-BT]

166. SMITH, W. C. S., 1823–1896

"1849 Journal of W. C. S. Smith: San José del Cabo to San Diego," edited by Harry W. Crosby. *Gold Rush Desert Trails to San Diego and Los Angeles in 1849*. San Diego, Calif.: Corral of the Westerners, 1995. Pp. 125–149. *A Journey to California in 1849*. Fairfield, Wash: Ye Galleon Press, 1984. First printed [1925?] in Napa, California. Also found in *A History of California: The America Period*, by Robert Glass Cleland. New York: The MacMillan Company, 1922. Pp. 483–495. The original manuscript, "Narrative of a 49-er–and incidents of travel from New York to San Francisco, 1849-1888," is held in the Mandeville Special Collections Library, University of California, San Diego.

Smith left New York January 15, 1849, on the bark *Eugenia*. After landing at Vera Cruz, he made his way to San Blas, where he boarded the condemned whaler *Mary Frances*, arriving in Mazatlán after "six days dull sailing and drifting." Another ten days brought the passengers to Cabo San Lucas, Baja, where he left the "floating coffin," feeling safer on foot and on terra firma. They started out on April 6 with a rudimentary map, thinking that "it would be but a pleasant horseback canter of some thirty or forty days to San Francisco." Instead, they began what was to become a tortuous and unforgettable trip that lasted the better part of ninety days. In spite of the rigors of travel, Smith managed to keep a daily journal, thus leaving an excellent and lengthy account of adventures on the peninsula.

In addition, Smith recounts his experiences in the mines and in the founding of the town of Marysville. He ultimately settled in Napa, California, where he ran a retail grocery business. This forty-niner attained a sort of fame on April 14, 1865, when Abraham Lincoln, in his last official act, appointed him collector of internal revenue for California's fifth district.

Harry Crosby is the foremost authority on the history of Baja, California, having spent years on archival and on-site research (*172*). Thus his expert editing of the Baja portion of the Smith diary adds a great deal of new material for study. He locates the mission trail accurately, while at the same time includes a number of his spectacular photographs. [MX-BJ]

167. VAN WINKLE, I. S., 1825–1881

"I. S. Van Winkle," by H. L. Van Winkle. *Quarterly, Society of California Pioneers* 5 (1928):139–147.

Van Winkle's son recalls that his father sailed from New York to Vera Cruz on the bark *Mara* and proceeded overland to Mazatlán. Van Winkle was among the investors in the *San Blasena* and stayed with her all the way to Monterey, California, where she landed on June 15 after sixty-five days at sea. The J. D. B. Stillman (*181*) and Daniel Woods (*169*) entries complement this story.

Van Winkle's son leaves us with a number of colorful vignettes, such as the time he was called upon to be the judge at a trial because he was the only one in town who owned a white shirt. This goldseeker found rich diggings on the Merced River and reported a $36,000 profit in one month. He later founded I. S. Van Winkle and Company in San Francisco and ran a mining supply business until his death. [MX-BT]

168. WINN, ALBERT MAVER, 1818–1883

"An Autobiography by William Watkins Winn, 1957." The Winn Family Papers (1858–1958) are in the Bancroft Library.

It is apparent that these reminiscences were intended to be a family history and genealogy for descendants, and there is little here to recreate the overland adventure. Winn was a frontiersman and soldier from Vicksburg, Mississippi, who joined an emigrant train promoted by Corpus Christi resident Henry Lawrence Kinney. Winn arrived in town on February 24, 1849, and started for Laredo with thirty-two companions. He found the going tough since the Comanches were a constant threat. Moreover, locating feed and water was a constant challenge. Winn eventually made it to Mazatlán. He had no money and very little else, so he managed to stow away on a bark for San Francisco, where he arrived on May 28, 1849.

According to Robert Livingston (1989:1–14), Winn entered politics, opened a business in Sacramento, and distinguished himself as a civic leader and humanitarian. A monument in Sacramento's city cemetery honors him as founder of the Order of the Native Sons of the Golden West and as the father of city government in Sacramento. [MX-BT]

169. WOODS, DANIEL B.

Sixteen Months at the Gold Diggings. New York: Harper and Brothers, 1852.

The Rev. Daniel B. Woods sailed out of Philadelphia on February 1, 1849, with the Camargo Company. The destination was Tampico, Mexico, where Woods wrote that they "went, not as spectators, but as actors upon its boards. The first night after our arrival, we appeared upon its stage, performing our parts in the celebrated farce, the California Gold Diggers—a play which has since been performed a thousand times, and with unabated interest" (p. 21). This group went to San Blas by way of Guadalajara, invested in the thirty-six-foot schooner *San Blasena*, then squeezed into that boat with inadequate provisions and a captain who had not been to sea in twenty years. Woods and four companions disembarked at Cabo San Lucas and found passage on the *Collooney*. I. S. Van Winkle (*167*) was one who remained on board the *Blasena*, while several other passengers headed for shore and risked a hike to San Diego. Edwin Allen Sherman (*165*) was one who helped organize the group.

The Woods story is a gold rush classic and a treat to read. The major portion of his book revolves around tales of success and failure in the California mining camps. [MX-BT]

MEXICAN GOLD TRAIL
REFERENCE WORKS

170. BROWNE, J. ROSS

Resources on the Pacific Slope. New York: D. Appleton and Company, 1869. "Explorations in Lower California," *Harper's New Monthly Magazine* 37 (October 1868): 9-23.

Author, artist, government agent, and adventurer, Browne traveled widely in the West, leaving memorable accounts accompanied by detailed and often humorous sketches of events and sites. The above accounts contain narrative descriptions of his 1867 exploration of the Baja peninsula, which include a history of the area and a statistical and descriptive summary of the mines and minerals, climate, topography, agriculture, commerce, and manufactures.

171. CROCKETT, C. F.

"Reported Loss of a Company from Newark," *Newark (N.J.) Daily Advertiser*, August 13, 1849.

Though Crockett started out with John Clark (*140*) and Samuel Crane (*141*), he apparently found his way to San Francisco by faster and safer means, arriving on June 30. He had heard some rumors about the *Dolphin* and feared his friends might have died. His report mainly deals with gold rush activities in San Francisco. [MX-BT]

172. CROSBY, HARRY W.

Last of the Californios. La Jolla, Calif.: The Copley Press, Inc., 1981. "El Camino Real in Baja California: Loreto to San Diego," *Journal of San Diego History* 23 (Winter 1977):1–45.

Crosby is one of the first to have searched for, mapped, and followed the old mission trail in Baja, and has provided a fine historical background to consult when studying the route of forty-niners. In addition, he furnishes good ethnographic material and superb photographs of the Baja terrain.

173. DODD, HORACE L., EDITOR

"A Comedy of Errors, a Chronicle of Survival," *Gold Rush Desert Trails to San Diego and Los Angeles in 1849.* San Diego, Calif.: Corral of the Westerners, 1995. Pp. 151–160.

Dodd has provided a new look at the saga of the *San Blasena* by comparing the stories of Daniel B. Woods (*169*), Charles M. Blake (*138*), and J. D. B. Stillman (*181*).

174. DUMKE, GLENN S.

"Across Mexico in '49," *Pacific Historical Review* 18 (1949): 33–44.

Dumke offers some reasons for choosing Mexican travel and compares and contrasts a variety of routes taken by the forty-niners. He makes no reference to the trip on the Baja peninsula.

175. EGAN, FEROL

The El Dorado Trail: The Story of the Gold Rush Routes Across Mexico. Lincoln: University of Nebraska Press, 1984. "Jornada del Muerto," *The American West* 6 (July 1969):12–19.

Ferol Egan has written about forty-niner travel on the various routes through Mexico. It is well researched and thoroughly readable. In addition, he has gone on site and can report on the terrain and confirm goldseekers' descriptions. He does not mention the trek up Baja.

176. ETTER, PATRICIA A.

"Ho! For California on the Mexican Gold Trail," *Overland Journal* 11 (1993):2–15. "Forty niners in the Land of the Aztecs," *Journal of Arizona History* 32 (Spring 1991):1–20. "Through Mexico in '49," *Bulletin of Bibliography* 46 (September 1989):147–159.

The first two articles deal with forty-niner experiences in Mexico including Baja, California. The third provides a brief annotated list of diaries and journals by many who attempted the Mexico crossing. Some of the material in this work has been adapted from the *Bulletin of Bibliography*.

177. FORBES, ?

A Trip to Mexico, or, Recollections of a Ten-Months Ramble in 1849–50, by a barrister. London: Smith, Elder, and Co., 1851.

The author sailed from Southampton, England, in the fall of 1849 for a ten-month pleasure trip to Mexico. His story contains some fine ethnographic material and vivid descriptions of the route the forty-niners followed between Vera Cruz, Mexico City, Puebla, Guadalajara, and Tepic.

178. GOHRES, HELEN, EDITOR

"Barefooted to the Gold-Fields," *Journal of San Diego History* 9 (July 1963):34–41.

The editor has unsuccessfully attempted to write the story of Louis Bonestell (*139*) and John Griffith (*149*) by paraphrasing segments from J. D. B. Stillman's *Seeking the Golden Fleece* (*181*).

179. M'ILVAINE, WILLIAM

Sketches of Scenery and Notes of Personal Adventure in California and Mexico. Foreword by Robert Glass Cleland. San Francisco: Grabhorn Press, 1951.

This fine book, more pictorial than narrative, contains sixteen lithographic plates recalling scenes from M'Ilvaine's travels across Mexico and his sojourn in California. He arrived in California by sea in June of 1849, then returned to New York via Acapulco, Mexico City, and Vera Cruz. This return trip is included because his colorful, descriptive, and intelligent text helps round out the story of travel in Mexico in 1849.

180. SHAW, DAVID AUGUSTUS

"An Account of the Sufferings of a Party of Argonauts who were Compelled to Abandon their Vessel 'The Dolphin' on the Peninsula of Lower California, and Make Their Way on Foot to San Diego," in *Eldorado or California as Seen by a Pio-*

neer, 1850–1900. Los Angeles: B. R. Baumgardt & Co., 1900. Pp. 299–313.

Shaw's last chapter bears the same title as the story J. D. B. Stillman recorded from John Griffith's diary in 1877 (*149*). In addition, it is evident that Shaw copied and/or paraphrased most of Stillman's work for this 1900 publication.

181. STILLMAN, J. D. B.

"Cruise of the Dolphin," in *Seeking the Golden Fleece: A Record of Pioneer Life in California.* San Francisco, 1877. Pp. 327–352. Microfiche. Louisville, Ky., Lost Cause Press, 19–. Nineteenth-century American literature and history. Series C. Trans-Mississippi West. "Cruise of the San Blasena," *The Overland Monthly* (September 1875): 241–248. Copied in *Gold Rush Desert Trails to San Diego and Los Angeles, 1849.* San Diego, Calif.: Corral of the Westerners, 1995. Pp. 154–159.

A number of individuals represented in this bibliography left reminiscences of time spent on the rotting hulk *Dolphin:* Samuel Crane (*141*); John Griffith (*149*); and Louis Bonestell (*139*). Stillman recreated the saga of the ship using Griffith's diary to illustrate the trip up the Baja peninsula.

For his second article, Stillman assembled the reminiscences of a number of forty-niners whose fortunes were closely tied to the schooner *San Blasena.* Arriving safely in San Blas after crossing central Mexico, and finding no available transportation to California, a group of men purchased the thirty-five-ton schooner. They crowded into the badly fitted and unseaworthy vessel on April 12, 1849, for a most tedious voyage. Diarists represented here, Daniel B. Woods (*169*) and I. S. Van Winkle (*167*), have written stories about the saga.

EPILOGUE

Though 150 years have passed, we continue to be fascinated with the gold rush to California, often referred to as the greatest mass migration in history. As pointed out in the Historical Overview, scholars have for the most part concentrated their studies on travel along the California and Oregon trails. I have also shown that lack of research on southern trails has resulted in their elimination from most published maps. Moreover, they are often incorrectly traced when they are shown. It is now time to become better informed about the evolution of southern trails if we are to fully appreciate their importance in the history of the westward movement.

There has been too much guesswork in the past about the location of the Southern, Apache Pass, and Gila trails. I have located and visited many of the sites over the past fifteen years, and more recently, the Oregon-California Trails Association (OCTA) has adopted a long-range goal to include the various emigrant trails comprising the Southern Route to California in the National Historic Trails system. To that end, members of Southwest OCTA have been in the field with emigrant diaries to help them look for landmarks and survey trail segments. Since the trails have been so long ignored, we find only vestiges in many areas due to erosion, overgrazing, road building, dam building, and urbanization. As a result, we hope to locate remaining segments and encourage future preservation, in addition to transferring as much information as possible to topographic maps so the findings will not be lost over time. These maps will be archived at OCTA's headquarters in

Independence, Missouri. In addition to assistance in defining trails, I hope that the 181 diaries and books listed here will provide a catalyst for future research into diverse areas such as ethnographic, environmental, subsistence, settlement, and other studies.

Reasons for taking the different trails varied, but the reasons for moving west were much the same. There had been hard times in the 1840s and emigrants went to make a fortune and return home as soon as they achieved that goal. The hoped-for riches would insure a better life for themselves and their families. Though it took courage to decide to start out on the 2,500-mile trip, golden reports in newspapers and promised government support for protection and roadbuilding made it easier for thousands to jump on the bandwagon. There was also the unspoken promise of excitement and adventure, which was lacking in the daily lives of many. In addition, there were a few who needed to escape the law and some who needed to get away from unhappy families.

It was a migration of many cultures and included American Indians and black men, both free and slave. John Forsyth may have predicted the future makeup of California when he awoke on November 20 and "arose from my Buffalo Robe beside my carreta," and looked around at his bedfellows. "Here lay a Mexican soldier with his Wife. There a huddle of Indians, all ages sexes & sizes & a little further on a few goldseekers with their Blue Blankets & comfortable Buffalo robes … thus in a small space on the American Desert slept different Nations, Languages & colors in perfect amity" (48).

These forty-niners were the forefront of migration to California, and in spite of difficulties of travel and hardships encountered in a new land, they found much more than gold—they found freedom to seek out a new destiny. And, as we have learned from these stories, many decided to stay in California and put their creative talents to work to build new lives for themselves and contribute to the growth of the state. This migration increased steadily over the years, and a burgeoning, diverse population from around the world continues to crowd the states' shores in a search for the golden dream.

APPENDIX

ROUTES OF THE FORTY-NINERS

The following lists are given to assist researchers who want to study aspects of a trail without having to browse through every account. Route #1 represents the "feeder" trails, while Route #2 covers the main trails: Southern, upper and Lower Gila, and Apache Pass trails. It also includes those who trod the Zuni–Salt River shortcut. Since all those individuals eventually connected with the lower Gila Trail at one point there is no separate listing for them. Similarly, there is no listing for those who trod across Mexico and sailed to California.

ROUTE #1
FORT SMITH-SANTA FE TRAIL [FS]
32 ACCOUNTS

Aldrich, Lorenzo D.
Anonymous
Blunt, Phineas Underwood
Boyles, John R.
Brownlee, Robert
Candee, J. G.
Chamberlin, William H.
Conway, Mary
Counts, George
Creighton, Mary Lee
Crumpton, Hezekiah John
Eliot, Robert
Fouts, D. Lambert/Ricks,
    Caspar Stinemets
Gooding, Larry
Goulding, William R.
Green, Robert B.

Hammond, John
Howard, David "Deacon"
Hoyt, John P.
Jordan, David
King, Alfred D.
King, Arthur
Lasselle, Stanislaus
May, John
Pattison, George K.
Ramsey, Wilberforce
Ricks, Caspar Stinemets/Fouts,
    D. Lambert
Shinn, Silas Monroe
Sniffen, George S.
Teller, Woolsey
Thibault, Frederick James
Woodruff, Alden M.

ROUTE #1
SANTA FE TRAIL [SF]
20 ACCOUNTS

Beckwith, Edward Griffin
Bouldin, James E.
Brainard, David
Brisbane, William
Chatham, J. W.
Collier, James
Deaderick, David A.
Forsyth, John Robert
Hayes, Benjamin Ignatius
Heslep, Augustus M.

Hudgins, John
Hunter, William W.
Pancoast, Charles Edward
Pennell, William Doyle
Powell, H. M. T.
Randall, Andrew
Simmons, Joseph R.
Stevens, Benjamin
Stuart, Jacob
Williams, R. G.

ROUTE #1
TEXAS TRAILS [TT]
19 ACCOUNTS

Beeching, Robert
Birt, Samuel P.
Blair, Charles M.
Brockway, H. S.
Cameron, John B.
Caperton, John
Cox, Cornelius
Demarest, David Durie
Eccleston, Robert
Harris, Lewis Birdsall

Hays , John Coffee
Hunter, Robert
Irby, Benjamin F.
Murchison, John
Nugent, John
Platt, "Silent"
Strentzel, John T.
Strentzel, Louisiana
Weed, L. N.

ROUTE #1
TEXAS TRAILS AND MEXICO [TM]
16 ACCOUNTS

Anonymous (2 accounts)
Duval, Isaac
Eastland, Joseph Green
Eastland, Thomas B.
Fairchild, John A.
Harris, Benjamin Butler
Hobbs, James
Hooper, H. O.

Huff, William P.
Knapp, W. Augustus
McGaffey, Joseph Wyatt
Patterson, George Washington
Pownall, Joseph
Robb, John S. "Solitaire"
Wood, Harvey

ROUTE #1
MEXICO VIA ALTAR [MX]
3 ACCOUNTS

Audubon, John Woodhouse
Bachman, Jacob Henry

Dawson, Nicholas "Cheyenne"

ROUTE #1
MEXICO VIA EL CAMINO
DEL DIABLO [DH]
3 ACCOUNTS

Dye, Job Francis
Hobbs, James

Hubbard, Cal

ROUTE #1
MEXICO VIA DURANGO [MX]
16 ACCOUNTS

Anonymous
Dunphy, William
Eastland, Joseph Green
Eastland, Thomas B.
Emerson, William Henry
Gunn, Lewis Carstairs
Hardin, Robert S.
Hooper, H. O.

Knapp, W. Augustus
McGaffey, Joseph Wyatt
McKnight, George
McNeil, Samuel
Patterson, George Washington
Patterson, Lawson, B.
Perkins, William
Winn, Albert Maver

ROUTE #1
MEXICO VIA TAMPICO [MX]
4 ACCOUNTS

Blake, Charles Morris
Sayre, Thomas

Sherman, Edwin Allen
Woods, Daniel B.

ROUTE #1
MEXICO VIA VERA CRUZ [MX]
12 ACCOUNTS

Anonymous (Caspar)
Baker, George Holbrook
Bonestell, Louis Henry
Clark, John R.
Crane, Samuel P.
Dodge, Henry Lee

Ferris, A. C.
Griffith, John W.
Jordan, Rudolph
Perry, J. A.
Smith, W. C. S.
Van Winkle, I. S.

ROUTE #1
FROM RIO GRANDE VIA MEXICOTRAILS TO SOUTHERN ENTRANCE, GUADALUPE PASS [MX]
5 ACCOUNTS

Clarke, Asa Bement
Durivage, John E.
Evans, George W. B.

Noble, Robert Watson
Wozencraft, Oliver M.

ROUTE #2
PIMA VILLAGES VIA ZUNI [ZU]
4 ACCOUNTS

Beckwith, Edward Griffin
Brisbane, William

Collier, James
Randall, Andrew

ROUTE #2
APACHE PASS TRAIL [AP]
5 ACCOUNTS

Caperton, John
Demarest, David Durie
Eccleston, Robert

Hays, John Coffee
Nugent, John

ROUTE #2
BAJA TRAIL [BJ]
8 ACCOUNTS

Blake, Charles Morris
Bonestell, Louis Henry
Clark, John R.
Crane, Samuel P.

Griffith, John W.
Hawks, James D.
Nye, William Foster
Smith, W. C. S.

ROUTE #2
UPPER GILA TRAIL
13 ACCOUNTS [GT]

Anonymous
Blair, Charles M.
Blunt, Phineas Underwood
Brockway, H. S.
Chamberlin, William H.
D. H.
Eliot, Robert

Green, Robert B.
Hammond, John
Howard, David "Deacon"
Hoyt, John P.
Lasselle, Stanislaus
Taylor, Joseph

ROUTE #2
SOUTHERN TRAIL [ST]
62 ACCOUNTS

Aldrich, Lorenzo D.
Anonymous (2 accounts)
Beeching, Robert
Birt, Samuel P.
Bouldin, James E.
Boyles, John R.
Brainard, David
Brownlee, Robert
Cameron, John B.
Candee, J. G.
Clarke, Asa Bement
Conway, Mary
Counts, George
Cox, Cornelius
Creighton, Mary Lee
Crumpton, Hezekiah John
Deaderick, David A.
Durivage, John E.
Duval, Isaac
Evans, George W. B.
Fairchild, John A.
Forsyth, John Robert
Fouts, D. Lambert/Ricks, Caspar
    Stinemets
Goulding, William R.
Harris, Benjamin Butler
Harris, Lewis Birdsall
Hayes, Benjamin Ignatius
Heslep, Augustus M.
Hudgins, John
Huff, William P.
Hunter, Robert

Hunter, William W.
Irby, Benjamin F.
Jordan, David
King, Alfred D.
King, Arthur
May, John
Murchison, John
Noble, Robert Watson
Pancoast, Charles Edward
Pennell, William Doyle
Platt, "Silent"
Powell, H. M. T.
Pownall, Joseph
Ramsey, Wilberforce
Ricks, Caspar Stinemets/Fouts,
    D. Lambert
Robb, John S. "Solitaire"
Shinn, Silas Monroe
Simmons, Joseph R.
Sniffen, George S.
Stevens, Benjamin
Strentzel, John T.
Strentzel, Louisiana
Stuart, Jacob
Teller, Woolsey
Thibault, F. J.
Weed, L. N.
Williams, R. G.
Wood, Harvey
Woodruff, Alden M.
Wozencraft, Oliver M.

GLOSSARY

Algodones Dunes, Imperial County, California: On crossing the Colorado River, travelers curved into Mexico to avoid a four-by-forty-mile stretch of sand featuring dunes as high as ninety feet.

Animas Mountains, Hidalgo County, New Mexico: Chain of mountains south of Lordsburg, close to the Mexican border.

Ben Moore Mountain, Grant County, New Mexico: See Soldier's Farewell.

Bent's Fort, Colorado: Charles Bent and Ceran St. Vrain built the fort in 1833 on the mountain branch of the Santa Fe Trail near modern La Junta. It became a center for Indian trade and stock raising, a rest spot for traders and travelers, and during the Mexican War, a rendezvous for explorers and the military.

Bowman, Sarah (Great Western): This remarkable woman was nicknamed after the largest steamship afloat at the time. She also had courage to match her size, since she was among the camp followers as General Zachary Taylor moved around in preparation for the war with Mexico. She moved on to Yuma some time around 1850, where she ran a brothel, saloon, and hotel. She died in 1866 and was buried with full military honors at the Fort Yuma cemetery.

Butterfield Pass, Maricopa County, Arizona: Vestiges of the trail are between Mobile and Gila Bend in the North Maricopa Mountains Wilderness. Location: USGS (T4S R2W Sec 28) Butterfield Pass Quadrangle, 1973.

Comanche Springs, Pecos County, Texas: Near the site of future Fort Stockton and a later stop on the Butterfield Trail, these were among the largest springs in Texas, later transformed to an Olympic-size swimming pool.

Cooke's Springs, Luna County, New Mexico: The site, northeast of Deming, is protected by the Bureau of Land Management. Location: USGS (T21S R8W Sec 23) Massacre Peak Quadrangle, 1964.

Coons' Ranch, Texas: Benjamin Franklin Coons, a St. Louis merchant, purchased the site, now in downtown El Paso, from Juan María Ponce de León in 1849, and built a tavern, stables, and store hoping to capitalize on hoped-for emigrant traffic. The place was also known as Franklin until 1852 when a post office was established under the name El Paso.

Corralitos, Chihuahua, Mexico: A small silver-mining town on the Janos road, which had been opened by an American, Robert McKnight.

Cow Springs, Luna County, New Mexico: See Ojo de Vaca.

Coyote Hills, Grant County, New Mexico: A group of low-lying hills about twenty miles south of the Muir exit from Interstate 10. Location: USGS (T26S R16W Sec 33) Brockman Hills Quadrangle, 1964.

Doña Ana, Doña Ana County, New Mexico: Spanish-Mexican settlement, five miles north of Las Cruces, founded in 1843. The village housed a U.S. Army detachment in 1849.

El Camino del Diablo (the Highway of the Devil): Starting at Caborca, Sonora, Mexico, the 250-mile trip by way of the Pinacate wilderness featured stops at Quitovac, Sonoyta, and Quito-vaquito, before moving toward Tule Tanks, Tinajas Altas, and Yuma across sere desert flats, lava malpais, and drifting sand. Hundreds died during summer, when waterholes dried up and temperatures soared to 120 degrees and more.

El Camino Real de Tierra Adentro (the Royal Road): An 1,800-mile trail connecting Taos, Santa Fe, and Mexico City. First blazed by Juan de Oñate in 1598, this is one of the oldest, longest, and most important highways in North America.

El Patrocinio, Baja, California: The rancho was a few miles north of mission San Jose de Gracia and had been in the custody of the Aguilar family since 1795. Ramon Aguilar was on hand to greet visitors in 1849, according to James Hawks (152:133).

Fort Davis National Historic Site, Jeff Davis County, Texas: The military post was established in 1854 to protect travelers on the Lower or Military Road from hostile tribes.

Foster's Hole, Sierra County, New Mexico: Named after Philip St. George Cooke's interpreter, Dr. Stephen C. Foster, who became the first alcalde of Los Angeles under the United States. The water hole is fifteen miles west of the Rio Grande. Location: USGS (T18S R6W Sec 36) Jug Canyon Quadrangle, 1989.

Garfield, Doña Ana County, New Mexico: Farming community ten miles northwest of Hatch on New Mexico 187, close to the place where emigrants left the Rio Grande. Information from the William Hunter diary was instrumental in locating the site. As a result, members of the Southwest Oregon-California Trails Association called the unnamed wash, "Hunter's Draw" (Tompkins 1996). Location: USGS (T17S R5W Sec 36) Garfield Quadrangle, 1961.

Guadalupe Pass, Hidalgo County, New Mexico: Located on the international boundary on the Arizona–New Mexico border, the trail was the main link between Chihuahua and missions in Sonora and Arizona. Location: USGS (T34S R21W Sec 16) Cienega Springs Quadrangle 1918.

Guadalupe Pass, Hudspeth County, Texas: The trail wound through Guadalupe Mountains National Park, Texas. This should not be confused with Guadalupe Pass in the Guadalupe Mountains on the Arizona–New Mexico border.

Hatcher, John L., ca.1812–ca.1897: A Virginia frontiersman, Hatcher went west about 1835 to work at Bent's Fort. He had lived with the Kiowas, served as Lieutenant James W. Abert's guide in the Texas Panhandle, and became an army scout during the Mexican War. He guided James Collier to California by way of Zuni in 1849. The guide retired to Oregon.

Horsehead Crossing, Texas: So named because skeletons of mules and horses littered both sides of this well-known Pecos River crossing at the Crane and Pecos county lines some twenty miles northwest of the town of Girvin. Indians stole them over time in Chihuahua. Thirsty after a hard drive, the animals often plunged into the river and drank until they became sick and died.

Hueco Tanks, El Paso County, Texas: An area of natural rock basins thirty-two miles east of El Paso that holds a reliable supply of rainwater. It had been a strategic travel stop for centuries. Here ancient petroglyphs and the names of forty-niners are etched side by side on the rocks.

Janos, Chihuahua, Mexico: Established in 1690, the presidio lies on modern Highway 10. In 1849, a road out of Janos linked the town with the Guadalupe Pass, Arizona trailhead.

Jornada del Muerto (Journey of Death), New Mexico: The ninety-mile waterless shortcut and main trading route to Chihuahua, which cut off the bend of the Rio Grande between San Marcial and Rincon, claimed the lives of numerous travelers over the years.

Kirker, James, 1793–1853: This colorful Irishman came to New Mexico in 1825. He worked in the Santa Rita mines, ran an Apache scalp-hunting business in Chihuahua, served as scout for

Doniphan between 1846 and 1848, and helped fight the Utes. He guided the Peoria (Illinois) Company to California in 1849 by way of the Southern Trail. He died in his cabin on Mount Diablo, California.

Las Vegas, San Miguel County, New Mexico: First settled in 1833, Las Vegas became a popular stop on the Santa Fe Trail. It earned a spot in the history books when General Stephen Watts Kearny and his Army of the West arrived in 1846. Kearny climbed to a rooftop overlooking the town plaza, proclaimed New Mexico Territory part of the United States, then raised the first American flag to fly in the territory.

Little River, Indian Territory (Oklahoma): James Edwards located his trading post on the right bank of Little River about one and a half miles north of where it flows into the Canadian, near modern Holdenville. There was a Seminole settlement nearby.

Llano Estacado (Staked Plains): Spreading over 30,000 square miles from west Texas to New Mexico, the vast semi-arid plain is treeless and features short grass as far as the eye can see.

Mariposa Indian War, California: As thousands of miners encroached on their territory, Indian tribes in the Sierra Nevada foothills became increasingly restless. Some 200 miners volunteered for the Mariposa Battalion in 1851 to help control and treat with the various tribes.

Maxwell, J. W.: On September 3, 1849, Maxwell wrote in the "Rancho Santa Ana del Chino Register Book" (*102*) that he was from Kaskaskia, Illinois and "am bound for California." He had guided E. A. Baldwin's Villa Onondaga Company from Fort Smith to California by way of Gila Trail. Both the *Arkansas State Democrat* (4/27/1849) and Grant Foreman (*116*:38) mistakenly wrote that this was his more famous cousin Lucien Bonaparte (also from Kaskaskia), who had served with Frémont, was friend and confidant to Kit Carson, and master of the famous Maxwell grant in New Mexico. J. W. was later credited with the discovery of a new trail to Yreka through the Scott Mountains, which was called Maxwell's Pass (Boggs 1942:195). Californians called him Captain Maxwell.

Mesón: A Mexican inn with a central plaza that housed both men and animals.

Murderer's Camp (Kenyon Station), Maricopa County, Arizona: Site of the Davis-Hickey feud and burial a half mile south of the Gila River. Location: USGS (T4S R7W Sec 36) Citrus Valley West Quad, 1973.

North Fork Town, Indian Territory: The Creeks settled this place about eighty miles west of Fort Smith in the vicinity of modern Eufala, Oklahoma.

Northern Mines, California: Refers to those mines in the Sierra Nevada foothills that were located between Downieville and Placerville.

Ojo de Vaca (Cow Springs), Grant County, New Mexico: These are on Cow Springs Ranch between Deming and Lordsburg. Location: USGS (T1S R20W Sec 7) Cow Springs Quadrangle, 1972.

Old Spanish Trail: The trail connected Santa Fe and Los Angeles; caravans took off annually with trade goods. The first expedition arrived in Los Angeles during the winter of 1829; the last recorded trip was in 1848. After leaving Abiquiu in the Chama River valley, pack trains passed over the Continental Divide in southwest Colorado; crossed the Colorado, Green, and Sevier rivers in Utah; entered the Great Basin; and then went south to Los Angeles by way of Las Vegas and Cajon Pass.

Oregon-California Trails Association (OCTA): Headquartered in Independence, Missouri, the organization is dedicated to the preservation, appreciation, and enjoyment of all the trans-Mississippi migration trails to the west. Maps from the Southern Trails project will be archived in Independence.

Papago Indians, Arizona: I have retained the term Papago as first choice for this work since that was the name commonly used for this group of American Indians until the mid 1980s, when the tribe officially became the Tohono O'odham Nation. The Spanish coined the term Papago (bean eaters), whereas the Indians called themselves Tohono O'odham (desert people).

Pima villages, Maricopa County, Arizona: Piman-speaking agriculturalists lived in these scattered villages along the Gila River near modern Sacaton.

Rancho Colorado, Baja, California: The ranch was about twenty miles south of mission San Luis Gonzaga. The proprietor was Portuguese Francisco Betancur, who had been on the peninsula since 1838 and counted his wealth in cattle and horses (Crosby 166:1995:143).

Raton Pass, Colorado/New Mexico: Numerous switchbacks at high altitudes challenged the traveler at the pass, which was on the mountain branch of the Santa Fe Trail. Though it was 100 miles longer than the Cimarron Cutoff, there was plenty of water and less exposure to Indian attack.

San Bernardino Rancho, Sonora, Mexico, and Cochise County, Arizona: An 1821 grant, which its owner, Lieutenant Ignacio Perez, abandoned in 1837, due to incessant Apache raids. Forty-niners had good luck hunting wild cattle here, descendants of the old San Bernardino herd. John Slaughter, cattleman and formidable sheriff of Cochise County, Arizona, bought the land in 1884.

San Jose del Cabo, Baja, California: A mission was established here in 1730 two miles from the beach, and according to W. C. S. Smith (166:24) supported a population of some 500. J. Ross Browne visited the town in 1868 (170:582–583) and found about 600 people, many of whom were employed in the sugar cane industry.

Soldier's Farewell Hill, Grant County, New Mexico: Lieutenant Emory named this mountain after his friend Ben Moore of the First Dragoons in 1846. The hill, at the southern end of the Burro Mountains and west of Deming, was renamed in 1856. Location: USGS (T22S R14W Sec 31) Soldier's Farewell Hill Quadrangle, 1980.

Southern Mines, California: Refers to mining camps in the Sierra Nevada foothills that were located between Placerville and Mariposa.

Todos Santos, Baja, California: In 1868, J. Ross Browne (170:748) said the town of white-washed adobe houses surrounded a church and plaza set in a broad, fertile arroyo, where sugar cane was the principal product.

Tohono O'odham Indians, Arizona: See Papago Indians.

Truth or Consequences, Sierra County, New Mexico: The town was known as Palomas Hot Springs until 1950, when it adopted the name of a well-known radio show. The town marks the approximate location where General Stephen Watts Kearny and the Army of the West left the Rio Grande.

Warner's Ranch, San Diego County, California: Once Jonothan Trumbull Warner was granted Mexican citizenship, he applied for some 49,000 acres in an area called Valle de San José, which he received in 1844. It was conveniently located on the Old Emigrant Trail at the fork of two roads—one leading to San Diego, the other to the pueblo of Los Angeles. He later became known as Juan José, and one who dispensed liberal hospitality to passers-by. The crumbling remains of the old adobe ranch house is a few feet from California 79, next to a bronze plaque informing passers-by that this is State Landmark 311.

Whitmire Pass, Hidalgo County, New Mexico: A low gap in the Animas Mountains on the west side of Playas Lake. Location: USGS (T29S R18W Sec 8) Whitmire Pass Quadrangle, 1982.

REFERENCES CITED

Anthony, C. V. *Fifty Years of Methodism: A History of the Methodist Episcopal Church*. San Francisco: Methodist Book Concern, 1901.

Bancroft, Hubert Howe. *The Works of Hubert Howe Bancroft: Popular Tribunals*, Vol. 2. San Francisco: The History Company, Publishers, 1887.

Brown, T. Allston. *History of the American Stage*. New York: Benjamin Blom, 1969.

Browne, J. Ross. *A Dangerous Journey*. Palo Alto Calif.: Arthur Lites Press. 1950.

California Artillery, 1st California Guard, 1849–(Militia). San Francisco, Sept. 26, 1850. Bancroft Library, F869.S3 C1473.

CKEC Constitution of the Knickerbocker Exploring Company of the City of New York. Manuscript with the William Goulding Diary, Yale Collection of Western Americana, Beinecke Rare Book and Manuscript Library, 1849.

CSL California State Library, California Information File.

CSJC *1850 Census of San Joaquin County California*. Stockton, Calif.: San Joaquin Genealogical Society, 1959.

Dallam, Richard. "Diary of Richard Dallam, Cattle Drover. Over the Trail from Texas to California . . . 1852-1864." Manuscript in the Yale Collection of Western Americana, Beinecke Rare Book and Manuscript Library.

Eldredge, Zoeth Skinner. *History of California*, Vol. 3. New York: The Century History Co., 1915.

Ellis, George M. Personal communication in the author's files, 1996.

Etter, Patricia A., Unpublished statistical study of Southern Route migration 1990-1996.

Guinn, J. M. *History of the State of California and Biographical Record of Coast Counties, California*. Chicago: The Chapman Publishing Co., 1904.

HAL, *History of Alameda County*. Oakland: M. W. Wood, 1883.

Haskins, C. W. *The Argonauts of California*. New York: Fords, Howard & Hulbert, 1890.

Hayden, Carl. Verification of Route of the Army of the West, 1846, E. O. 061.01 dated June 15, 1937, Fort Sam Houston, Texas. Carl Hayden Papers, MSS #1, Box 782, folder 1, Department of Archives and Manuscripts, University Libraries, Arizona State University, Tempe.

HNL *History of Napa & Lake Counties California*. San Francisco: Slocum Bowen & Co., 1881.

HTC *A History of Tuolumne County California*. San Francisco: B. F. Alley, 1882.

Ingersoll, Luther A. *Ingersoll's Century Annals of San Bernardino County, 1769–1904*. Los Angeles: L. A. Ingersoll, 1904.

Irvine, Leigh H., *History of Humboldt County, California*. Los Angeles: Historic Record Company, 1915.

Jackson, Donald Dale. *Gold Dust*. New York: Alfred A. Knopf, Inc., 1980.

Kemble, Edward C. *A History of California Newspapers 1846-1848*. Reprinted from the supplement to the *Sacramento Union* of December 25, 1858. Los Gatos, Calif.: The Talisman Press, 1962.

Livingston, Robert D. "A. M. Winn: Father of City Government in Sacramento." *Golden Notes* 35 (Fall 1989):1-14.

Mattes, Merrill J., *Platt River Road Narratives*. Urbana: University of Illinois Press, 1988.

MBHCM *A Memorial and Biographical History of the Counties of Merced, Stanislaus, Calaveras, Tuolumne, Mariposa, California*. Chicago: The Lewis Publishing Company, 1892.

MHTC *A Modern History of Tulare County*. Visalia, Calif.: Limited Editions of Visalia, Inc., 1974.

Milliken, Ralph L. "The Saga of Tom Hildreth—The Man Who Fed the California '49ers," *California Historian* 11 (March 1965):100–105.

Milner, Clyde, Carol A. O'Connor, and Martha A. Sandweiss. *The Oxford History of the American West*. New York: Oxford University Press, 1994.

Peters, Harry T. *California on Stone*. Garden City, N.Y.: Doubleday, Doran & Company Inc., 1935.

Ridge, Martin. *Atlas of American Frontiers*. San Francisco: Rand McNally, 1993.

Ross, Margaret, Personal communication in the author's files, 1984.

Smith, Ralph A. "Scalp Hunters in the Borderlands, 1835-1850," *Arizona and the West* 6 (Spring 1964):17.

Stewart, George R. *The California Trail*. New York: McGraw Hill, 1962.

Swift, Gustavus. Letter to California State Library, November 2, 1951. Manuscript in the California Information File, Sacramento, California.

Thompson, Thomas H., and Albert A. West. *History of Los Angeles County*. Oakland, Calif.: Thompson & West, 1880.

Thrapp, Dan L. *Encyclopedia of Frontier Biography*. Glendale, Calif.: The Arthur H. Clark Company, 1988.

Tompkins, Rose Ann. Personal communication in the author's files, 1996.

Unruh, John D. *The Plains Across*. Urbana: University of Illinois Press, 1979.

Index